SMALL PARTS
IN
HISTORY

SMALL PARTS IN HISTORY

Sam Llewellyn

BARNES
&NOBLE
BOOKS
NEW YORK

I am grateful to Tim Phillips, Patrick Sadd, Tom Studdaford, and
Prisca Laiter for their invaluable assistance in compiling this book.

First published in Great Britain in 1985
by Sidgwick & Jackson Limited, London.

This edition published by Barnes & Noble, Inc.,
by arrangement with the author.
1992 Barnes & Noble Books

ISBN 1-56619-029-0

Printed and bound in the United States of America

M 9 8 7 6 5 4 3 2 1

Contents

Introduction

History is full of little people. Behind great characters and events, a huge rabble swarms. And every now and then, a member of that rabble does something that sets in motion a chain of causes that leads to a great event.

So far, the rabble has been overlooked. But now its time has come. From now on, members of the rabble are known as Small Parts.

What (you may say) do you mean, Small Parts?

A Small Part is an insignificant historical character whose actions have significant historical consequences.

The ideal Small Part is a person who lives a life of perfect obscurity on a collision course with Destiny. Having collided, he or she then moves back into obscurity.

There are no specific qualifications for becoming a Small Part. You may be active or passive, energetic or supine. In this book are the accident-prone and the meticulous, courtiers and conspirators, gigolos and con men, sportspeople and lawyers, bums and buccaneers. All they have in common is that at some point in their lives, they became the falling pebble that caused a landslide.

Collecting Small Parts has problems of its own. By their very nature, they are sketchily recorded if they are recorded at all. Also, the landslides of history are so many that there may be disagreement about who started which one. And finally, any collection of Small Parts will be at best a random dip into history – for a definitive collection would be no more or less than a universal biography of every man, woman and child who has ever lived.

Looking for Small Parts has its rewards. Once you start, you find that your senses are sharpened and that new Small Parts pop up where you had previously noticed none. Another is that it lends a pleasant randomness to history, hitherto wrapped in strait-jackets by a succession of philosophers. Mind you, if the scholars get hold of Small Parts there is no telling what may happen.

For the day of the Small Part is with us as never before. Never before has the individual been so deeply submerged in the mass of humanity. All the signs are that history, having begun with the Small Part who first stood erect and brandished a bone tool, will end with another deep in a bunker, thumb hovering over a button, waiting for the order to play the last Small Part of all.

A little neglect may breed mischief . . . for want of a nail, the shoe was lost; for want of a shoe the horse was lost; and for want of a horse the rider was lost.

Benjamin Franklin

Agostino di Duccio

Who gave Michelangelo the lump

There are special places in history reserved for those who, through their mistakes, pave the way for genius. One of these places is reserved for the minor Renaissance Man Agostino di Duccio.

Like many other Florentines of the Renaissance, Agostino spent part of his youth as a mercenary soldier. Home from the wars, he began developing the other side of his nature, in approved Renaissance Man style, by taking up sculpture. His first independent work is the altar of Modena Cathedral. Having finished this in 1442 he returned to Florence, and demonstrated yet another side to his character when he was forced to leave town in a hurry having been arraigned with his brother on a church-looting charge.

Nearly twenty years later he returned to Florence. In the interim he had acquired a modest reputation for reliefs in the Attic style. The air of his home then inspired him to have a shot at something new on the Renaissance Man front. He ordered a very expensive eighteen-foot chunk of pure white marble from the famous quarries of Carrara. When it arrived, he complained that it was somehow the wrong shape. In the studio he managed to make it absolutely the wrong shape, by gouging a mighty chasm up its middle. He abandoned the project, left the lump of stone in the builder's yard of the Operai dell'Opera del Duomo – the Board of Works of the Cathedral – and died in 1481.

In 1501, the young Michelangelo Buonarroti was searching for a bit of marble from which to manufacture a statue to commemorate Florence's new Republican constitution. His friend Pier Soderini, knowing him to be short of funds, and being intimate with the Board of Works, gave him the Agostini Lump, which everybody had until then considered entirely wrecked. From it Michelangelo sculpted his

David, using the Agostino Overgouge as the space between the young giant-slayer's legs. The *David* was the work which brought Michelangelo his first recognition.

2

Richard Ameryk

Who really christened America

It has always been a matter of pride to Italian-Americans that their country gets its name from Amerigo Vespucci. Research shows that this pride is based on a fallacy: America is not called after Vespucci, but after the merchant Richard Ameryk of Bristol, England.

Ameryk – ap Maryk, or 'son of Merrick' in Welsh – seems to have been one of the pack of merchants who made Bristol England's second city in the late Middle Ages. He first swims into the ken of history in 1470, while engaged in a little real estate speculation involving the purchase of a third of the manorial lands of Clifton, and a good deal of the village of Long Ashton. This brought him into contact with other Bristol entrepreneurs, including the pushy John Cabot, who had a bee in his bonnet about an island provisionally called New Brasil which lay reasonably near Japan, a few thousand miles west across the Atlantic.

This was an attractive speculation of the kind Ameryk very much enjoyed. It was already known that large quantities of cod lay in those parts, and where cod was wealth could not be far behind. Ameryk therefore chipped in as principal backer of Cabot's expeditions. Cabot was a rapid and inventive talker, and a sound judge of human nature. (He had already inveigled several friars into taking part in the expedition, on the understanding that they would be allotted mighty bishoprics in the New World, when discovered.) In Ameryk's case, he presumably judged that what a hard-nosed self-made man wanted was money and immortality, not necessarily in that order. He therefore promised him large quantities of cod, gold, etc. and vowed in addition to name the new land after him. (It is interesting that the Ameryk crest, three mullets with bars, bears a marked similarity to the stars and stripes.)

3

The fact that Ameryk agreed to this deal is supported by the existence until the early nineteenth century of a calendar of Bristolian events for 1497, which deals with the Cabots' discovery of America — *mentioning America by name*. Yet the name did not come into general use in the rest of Europe for some ten years afterwards.

Italian-Americans who feel let down by these revelations can console themselves with the fact that both Cabot and Christopher Columbus were of Italian extraction. If they really want to commemorate national heroes, rather than colonialist financiers, they can always call their country Columbia; or, perhaps more accurately, and certainly more appropriately for the inhabitants of the northeast, Cabottia.

Charles Babbage

Victorian computer expert

Charles Babbage reverses the usual tendency of Small-Part players. Had he lived in the twentieth century, he would probably have been ranked alongside Einstein in the public esteem. But, unfortunately for him, he was born a hundred years too early, in Devonshire in 1792.

While at school he taught himself algebra, and spent much of his time teaching his teachers. On arrival at Cambridge he met Herschel, the astronomer. Thanks to this he left Cambridge without honours, since Herschel was a certainty to walk off with the mathematics prizes so Babbage, who had a deep-rooted dislike of coming second, refused to compete.

After leaving Cambridge he built a model calculating machine which in 1882 won him the Gold Medal of the Astronomical Society. Inspired by its success, he proposed another, larger machine, which he called the Difference Engine. The government, realizing its usefulness in the compiling of navigational tables, gave him a research grant of £1500. Babbage worked on the machine for four years in a state of increasing frenzy.

In 1828, the Duke of Wellington visited the works. Impressed, he authorized further finance and, for a time, Babbage's work proceeded smoothly. Then came a hitch. Babbage's nimble intellect had conceived a better, more powerful engine, which could perform just about any function asked of it. This he named the Analytical Engine, and it rendered the Difference Engine obsolete even before it had been built. Patriotic as ever, Babbage sent the specifications for his new machine to the government, inquiring at the same time whether the old one was still wanted.

This presented the government with a bit of a poser. For one thing, it had already spent a lot of money. For another, by this time nobody in government understood a word Babbage said, though there was a vague consensus that he was dashed able. In accordance with the policy of all governments before and since, they simply didn't answer his letters and strung him out for a record filibuster of eight years before telling him the project was scrapped.

The specifications for the Analytical Engine were extraordinarily advanced. It could perform complicated mathematical and logical operations. It was programmable with punched cards. It communicated with the outside world via a printer. It was, in fact, a perfectly good computer, some hundred and twenty years before its time. Its impact on the nineteenth century mind is neatly expressed in the following quotation from the *Dictionary of National Biography*: 'This extraordinary monument of inventive genius remains, and will doubtless forever remain, a theoretical possibility.' Tell that to IBM.

Babbage was somewhat discouraged by all this. He lived out the last thirty years of his life surrounded by the wreck of his engines in workshops attached to his house. Instead of visiting cards, he used cog wheels from his inventions, bearing his name in red paint. During his final years he devoted himself to a campaign against itinerant organ grinders, then plentiful in London, on the grounds that the disturbance they caused had robbed him of a quarter of his working life.

On his death, the larger chunks of mechanical debris in his workshop were removed to the Science Museum in Kensington where they may be observed today.

Dr Bell

A piece of elementary detection

Dr Bell, the prototype of the world's greatest fictional detective, was one of the last of a long line of doctors and surgeons who practised in Edinburgh during the hundred and fifty years preceding the turn of the century. He entered Edinburgh University at the age of sixteen, took his degree at twenty-one and was soon a highly regarded surgeon and teacher of surgery at the Royal Infirmary.

He was thin and wiry, dark, with an aquiline face, grey eyes and a jerky walk. It was noted that when a patient stepped into his consulting room he would fire a string of brusque questions, his eyes meanwhile flicking from the patient's hands to his shoes, noting callosities of the skin, worn patches on the clothes and little irregularities of gait and discourse. The doctor himself was well dressed according to the sombre fashion of the late nineteenth century. In later life, however, a very slight absent-mindedness in his dress, in the matter of worn trouser seats and a shoe cut by over-hasty application of the boot boy's scraping-knife, might have conveyed to the observant that he was now a widower, cared for not by a wife but by a housekeeper.

He was indeed widowed at the age of thirty-seven, and became (to those who did not know him) a pawky, rather daunting figure. Former members of Highland regiments in plain clothes were surprised to find their past careers an open book to Dr Bell, who could detect the military swagger a mile off. For Dr Bell's hobby was observation. Indeed, so sharp-eyed was he that many of his victims considered him to be a magician. He supplemented his talents with the study of graphology and the various soils surrounding Edinburgh.

In later life, he was often 'borrowed' by police investigating murder cases. During the Jack the Ripper killings, Bell and a friend each agreed to conduct an independent line of inquiry, to place their results in a sealed envelope, and to compare them – on the principal that if two men are looking for the same golf ball, and search for it according to their own methods and clues, they are twice as likely to find it as a single searcher. They both came up with the same result and sent it to Scotland Yard. The name of their Ripper was never disclosed but a week later, the murders ceased abruptly.

Dr Bell had many famous students, among them J. M. Barrie, Robert Louis Stevenson, and Arthur Conan Doyle. Stevenson, in self-imposed exile upon Samoa, wrote to Conan Doyle after he had read the first Sherlock Holmes story. 'Only one thing troubles me,' said Stevenson, speaking of the Great Detective. 'Can this be my old friend Joe Bell?'

It was.

When Conan Doyle was one of England's least successful oculists and was attempting to pay the milk bill via detective literature, it was Bell whom he chose as the model for his hero. And Sherlock Holmes inspired Hercule Poirot, the Continental Op, Sam Spade, the Harts and every other detective story since 1900.

Hans Brinker

The most important thumb in history

If we believe that we'll believe ANYTHING

The definitive Small Part is probably Hans Brinker's, the Dutch boy known to some as the Hero of Haarlem. His value to students lies not only in the fact that his slight deed saved countless acres of Holland from inundation, but also that nobody knows when he lived (or indeed, if he lived at all).

This is how the story goes. Brinker was a sunny-haired youth, offspring of a man whose job was to raise and lower sluice-gates in order to make the Dutch countryside wetter or drier, according to the dictates of crops and canal traffic. The kind-hearted youth one day took some cakes to a blind man who lived a few kilometres along the dyke. As he was returning home in the gathering dusk, he heard the gurgle of water. The fluid was seeping from a hole in the dyke. He immediately thrust in his forefinger, described in all accounts as 'chubby', staunched the flow and commenced yelling for help. None came.

All night he remained at his post, hollering. In the morning, still plugged in, he was spotted by a priest who alerted the maintenance crews. Brinker became a hero – not least, later, to the Dutch Tourist Office, who have erected a statue to him in Haarlem, which people come to see from all over the world.

This story is open to doubt. Brinker's finger may have been chubby, but in order to mend a breaking dyke it would have had to be as chubby as a couple of truckloads of clay. Dutch people are deeply ashamed of the story. But to the rest of the world, fat-fingered Brinker has come to embody the dogged Dutch spirit and the creative powers of Tourist Authorities.

Thomas Britton

The cultured coalman of Clerkenwell

On first consideration Thomas Britton seems an unlikely candidate for immortality. He was born in Northamptonshire for a start. During the last quarter of the seventeenth century he came to Clerkenwell, where he set up as a coalman. Clerkenwell had many secondhand bookshops, and Britton, who was of a literary bent, shuffled around them, sack on back, chatting with the proprietors and acquiring in the process considerable erudition and several influential friends.

Britton was considered to be an odd sort of coalman. He was often accused of sorcery, atheism and being a Jesuit as a result of the uncoalmanlike company he kept. It was this company that finally brought about his undoing. In 1714 there arrived among the throng at his small house a ventriloquist, keen to demonstrate his art. The ventriloquist caused his voice to emanate from an empty part of the room, instructing Britton to prepare for his death. Greatly struck, Britton took to his bed and expired within the week.

He had had a lifelong passion for music. One day, at a gathering of music-lovers organized by the violinist John Bannister, he had a bright and simple idea. If he were to invite a group of music-lovers to his house on a regular basis, and charge them a small annual fee to cover the expenses of the musicians, a good time would be had by all. These gatherings soon became extremely popular. Britton had invented not only the concert, but the season ticket.

Angela Burdett-Coutts

The millionairess who founded the chippie

A figure vital to the British national diet is Angela Burdett-Coutts, who in 1837 at the age of twenty-three inherited a sum of money equivalent to 13½ tons of gold. Wealth brought her no real happiness; she was of a retiring nature, keener on doing good works than on whooping it up with the suitors and fortune-hunters who formed queues wherever she went. When she did decide to get married in 1847, she summoned the Duke of Wellington to her house and proposed to him. He turned her down on the grounds that he was too old for her.

Towards the end of a life dedicated to philanthropy and, as a sideline, the care of parrots, she married William Bartlett who was several years younger than her and entirely unsuitable, against the advice of her friends, among whom were Charles Dickens and Queen Victoria. Her husband helped her through her mighty fortune. She died, surrounded by parrots, in 1906.

Her achievements were many. She wrote a manual of household management, a sort of poor woman's *Mrs Beeton*, with cheap but nourishing receipts and notes on weekly expenditure for the labouring man. She also contributed a quarter of a million pounds to purchase seed potatoes for Ireland, and had a hand in the reform of the nursing profession after the shambles of the Crimean War. Hers was also the keen perception that first observed the possibilities of two types of takeaway food shops in the East End of London, where she spent much time during the mid-nineteenth century. One type, of French origin, sold fried potatoes. The other, British to the core, sold fried fish. Why (asked Angela) should the two not be combined, to provide a balanced diet for the British working man?

Charles-Hippolyte de la Bussière

The human wasp

Charles-Hippolyte 'Delperch' de la Bussière, arguably the most significant figure in the French Revolution, began his career as a soldier but found his craving for the joyous life stronger than his martial zeal. Moving to Paris, he took up with a cheerful type of companion and earned a living as an actor, specializing in the portrayal of idiots. Offstage he kept himself amused during the grim early days of the Revolution by organizing practical jokes. He generally directed his pranks against the fiercer Revolutionary orators, particularly the Jacobins. Realizing just in time that he had made the wrong enemies at the wrong moment, he took nimble evasive action and got a job at the Committee of Public Safety.

Here he worked under the Public Prosecutor, the well-known shortener of aristos Fouquier-Tinville. His duties included copying out the dossiers of the arraigned, which would then be used as evidence for the prosecution at their trials. Faced with the river of paper, de la Bussière seems to have decided to be true to his non-Revolutionary past, and in the process stepped into History. Most dossiers he copied and passed on to the tribunals, as instructed. But some he shredded, chewed up and swallowed, leaving the tribunals without evidence and saving the subjects from the big knife. Later, growing more confident, he took to damping the wads of evidence to pulp, jamming them into his coat pockets and disposing of them by flicking them in pellet form through a bath-house window and into the Seine.

Among the 1153 lives he saved in this way were many minor poets and most of the actors of the Théâtre Française. (His only recorded slip-up is in the case of the great actor Larive, his long-time *bête noire*, in whose case he managed to masticate not the death warrant

13

but the notice of acquittal.) De la Bussière would have remained a plucky but insignificant figure had he not devoured the death warrant of Josephine de Beauharnais, later Empress of France. He was eventually arrested, but had been in prison for only eight days when Robespierre fell and he was freed.

Subsequently he returned to obscurity, his health wrecked nominally by syphilis but more probably by the tons of paper through which he had munched during his three and a half months at the Committee of Public Safety. His grateful rescuees organized a benefit performance at the Théâtre de la Porte St Martin, which was attended by the no less grateful Empress and Napoleon Bonaparte, her Emperor. The benefit raised 14,000 francs, 1000 of which came from Josephine herself. This sum de la Bussière, by now haggard, scrofulous and gibbering, spent in a matter of weeks. Soon afterwards, he died in a lunatic asylum.

The consequences of his career as a combination of the Scarlet Pimpernel and a human wasp are enormous not only for the artistic continuity of the French theatre, but also for the history of Europe as a whole. Not only was the Empress Josephine a soothing influence on Napoleon, restraining him from doing even more fearful damage, but she was also instrumental in engineering the marriage which produced Napoleon III, the Second Empire, and finally the Franco-Prussian War of 1870. Had there been no Franco-Prussian War there would in all probability have been no annexation of Alsace-Lorraine by the Germans. The ownership of these provinces was to be a bone of contention between France and Germany until 1945. . .

Had it not been for the mastications of de la Bussière, there might have been no First and Second World Wars.

Lucrezia Buti

The unfrocked nun

It is frequently said that behind every great man there is a good woman. The woman is seldom as good as Lucrezia Buti, who was the inspiration for the painter Fra Filippo Lippi and a nun. Born in 1433, she had entered the convent partly of her own free will and partly because after her father's death her brother could not be bothered to rustle up a dowry for her or her sister.

The convent was Santa Maria, Prato, in Florence. In 1456, the painter Fra Filippo Lippi was appointed chaplain to the convent, a move akin to sending a chimpanzee to guard a banana store. Just as Buti had become a nun more or less by accident, Lippi had become a monk solely because he had been brought up in a monastic orphanage. He was what is generally described as temperamentally unfitted for the religious life. By the age of fifty, when he had arrived at Prato, he had caroused his way round every cathouse on the Mediterranean littoral.

The Mother Superior asked Lippi to paint a fresco representing the Madonna della Sintola. Lippi agreed, and told her that he wished to use Buti as a model. He did not tell her that he had conceived a violent passion for Buti. The Mother Superior agreed, but specified a chaperone, so Buti and the beast would not be alone together. Lippi talked her out of it, thereby proving that like other Renaissance men he combined rhetorical gifts with his pictorial talents.

Shortly before the fresco was completed, Buti found herself pregnant. On 1 May 1456, Lippi, never one to let 'I dare not' wait upon 'I would', kidnapped her. The convent was astonished, not to say furious. Lippi once again plied his nimble tongue, however, and managed to keep his job as chaplain, though he deemed it inadvisable actually to turn up for work.

15

In due course, Buti gave birth to a son, known as Filippino. She had not much liked her previous cloistered life, but compared to the combination of young motherhood and the non-stop advances of the podgy Lippi, the convent must have looked like a holiday camp. In December 1458, she was back at Prato asking the Abbess to let her back in, and renewed her vows, ironically enough, in front of the picture of the Madonna della Sintola.

At this the convent finally sacked Lippi. Lippi asked for dispensation to marry Buti. This was granted, thanks to pressure from the Medicis, Lippi's patrons. Buti was once again sprung, and they set up house together, but once again, togetherness failed to bring perfect felicity. In 1467, Lippi was poisoned by a husband he had cuckolded and Buti vanished into the mists of history.

Buti's importance is not only that she acted as model for the paintings generally recognized as establishing Lippi as one of the supreme masters of the Quattrocento. It is also that it seems to be under the influence of their forbidden romance and subsequent tribulations that Lippi moved away from the static style of the earlier Renaissance, and into one full of life and movement that inspired (among others) the mighty Botticelli.

Captain Robert Byerly

New blood on the tracks

Thoroughbred horses are the result of crossing English mares with Arab stallions. The first Arab to be used in this way was the Byerly Turk. The Turk was originally an Ottoman cavalry charger. He was captured by the Austrians at the Siege of Buda in 1686, the turning point in the long wars of Christian against Turk in Central Europe. Three years later he was imported into England by Captain Robert Byerly of Byerly Hall, Yorkshire, who rode him in the Battle of the Boyne the following year.

In 1691, this battle-hardened paragon retired from active service and entered the lists of love. At stud he begat Jigg who begat Partner, who begat Tartar, who begat Herod. Through Herod, the Byerly Turk bloodline became the most important on the turf – particularly in England and France. His offspring includes Levmoss, winner of the 1969 Ascot Gold Cup.

Perhaps more important is the fact that importation of the Byerly Turk set a trend for crossing Arabs into the bloodline. Following the example set by Byerly, the Darley Arabian and the Godolphin Arabian (imported in 1704 and 1730 respectively) completed the trio from which all the thoroughbred horses in the world trace their descent.

James Byers

Muse among the ruins

James Byers was a Scot of the classical type and is responsible for the greatest history book in the English language. At the age of eighteen, he left Edinburgh, the Athens of the North, for the Rome of the South. Rome, in fact. Here he set himself up as a full-time classicist and occasional dealer in antiquities. (He was at one time the owner of the Portland Vase, a precious jug which then passed to Sir William Hamilton, British Ambassador at the court of Naples and husband of Lord Nelson's Emma.) He earned part of his living by lecturing on classical art and history to sprigs of the nobility and gentry having their minds stretched and their livers hardened by the Grand Tour.

During the second week in October 1764 he was presented with an odd client. This person was by turns moody and over-excited. As Byers conducted him round the eternal city, the client alternated between long silences and fits of almost uncontrollable gibbering. The week drew on; the client became increasingly wild-eyed. The itinerary for 15 October included the Capitol. Halfway through his spiel, Byers looked round, and saw that the client was seated on a broken column staring into space. Byers offered him a penny for his thoughts. The client apologized for his inattention, and offered as an excuse the fact that he was thinking about a book he had just decided to write.

The client was, of course, Edward Gibbon. As he wrote in his autobiography: 'It was at Rome, on the 15th October 1764, as I sat musing amidst the ruins of the Capitol . . . that the idea of writing the decline and fall of the city first started in my mind.'

The Decline and Fall of the Roman Empire is by common consent the greatest historical work in English literature. Without Mr Byers, it might never have come about. It is therefore appropriate that in

1785 he was made an Honorary Fellow of the Society of Anti-
quaries, and died after a distinguished old age in his native
Edinburgh.

Pierre-Jacques-Etienne Cambronne

Generally speaking. . .

Highly competent professional soldiers are often famous during their lifetimes, but it is rare that they make their mark on history. An exception to this rule is Pierre-Jacques-Etienne Cambronne, who taught the French to swear.

He joined the French army at the time of the Revolution in 1789, and rapidly proved himself to be a good officer. At the battle of Zurich in 1799, he acquitted himself with such bravery that he was offered the title of First Grenadier of France. He refused it with the tight-lipped modesty that was eventually to make him immortal.

When Napoleon was exiled to Elba, Cambronne accompanied him at the head of a division of the Old Guard. On Napoleon's return from Elba, Cambronne signed the address to the French Army summoning its soldiers to return to the standard. But it was at the Battle of Waterloo that he did that something extra that propelled him into History.

Towards the end of the battle, his Old Guard were surrounded by the enemy on all sides. An English voice rang out in a brief hush, demanding that he surrender. Victorian history books would have it that Cambronne, making use of the epigrammatic gifts available to all Frenchmen in emergencies, replied, 'La Garde meurt, elle ne se rend pas' – 'The Old Guard does not surrender, it dies.' Research now reveals that these words were not Cambronne's, but were uttered by a posterity-conscious major in one of the shattered squares.

What Cambronne actually said was 'Merde!'

Hitherto, this word had been more popular as a technical term than as an oath. But Cambronne's use of it to sum up his views of the greatest military defeat of the age catapulted it into a new significance. From then on, there was no looking back.

Cambronne was left for dead on the field of Waterloo, but he recovered, was taken to England and eventually died in his native Nantes. Statistics show that thanks to his sound popularizing work, his utterance is now one of France's five most popular cuss-words.

Captain Carey

The junior officer who scuppered the Empire

When republics are under discussion, the one that springs most readily to mind is France. It is not generally known that France is only a republic thanks to an embarrassing incident that occurred in South Africa to one Captain Carey.

Carey was born in 1847, and after a bilingual education in French and English joined the British army. He served in Jamaica and Central America – where he was involved in a curious incident. While escorting a civil official sent to parley with rebellious Indians, his party was attacked by these Indians. Escort and official became separated; the official was killed. Questions were asked but there was no conclusive evidence of dereliction of duty, and Carey's career continued.

In time he returned to Europe, and volunteered as a medical assistant in the Franco-Prussian War, succouring the wounded of both sides. At the outbreak of the Zulu War in 1879 he was sent to South Africa with reinforcements for the 24th Foot and acquired the reputation of being a useful staff officer. Among his duties was that of surveying the route for the march on the Zulu capital of Ulundi, and the provision of an escort for the Prince Imperial, graduate of the Royal Military Academy, Woolwich.

The Prince Imperial was the son of Napoleon III, exiled from France and now resident in tedious (but non-dangerous) Chislehurst, Kent, under the protection of the British government. The Prince had come to South Africa in order to prove his military prowess – something he deemed vital if he was to return to France and revive its imperial glories. He was indeed a brave and dashing young man, much given to galloping after Zulus waving a sword that had belonged to his illustrious forebear Napoleon I, apparently unaware

22

that this was by no means a British thing to do. He also seemed unaware that politically he was a hot potato of a type that the British command could well have done without, and that his propensity for dangerous Zulu-chasing was causing worry.

Captain Carey's brief, on taking charge of the Prince, was to keep him out of trouble. This he signally failed to do. On 1 June, while on an elementary surveying job, Carey, Prince and escort were attacked by about forty Zulus who had been hiding in the long grass. All would have been well had the Prince's girth not broken; he was hurled to the ground and separated from his sword. As the rest of the escort continued its hot retreat, the Prince was assegaied seventeen times. His attackers refrained from disembowelling his corpse, on the grounds that he had put up a good fight. This was little consolation for Carey.

The court martial found Carey guilty of dereliction of duty. The conviction was later quashed, largely because nobody could decide whether Carey or the Prince had been in charge of the escort. This did not stop the Empress Eugenie, and most of the French, blaming Carey. The affair broke him, but he continued in the army. In 1883, he died in Karachi when a wagon-horse kicked him in the groin.

Carey's achievement is to have presided over the extinction of the Bonaparte line. If the Prince Imperial had returned to France, there is every possibility that this young and dashing soldier would have captured the public imagination and been returned to power.

Sir George Cayley

Founder of the world's favourite airline (failed)

Sir George Cayley (1773-1857) invented the aeroplane and master-minded the first manned flight in a heavier-than-air machine. He was forgotten almost as soon as he was dead.

He was a Yorkshire baronet of an inquiring temperament. When he was nineteen he built a model helicopter from whalebone, and shortly afterwards he discovered the principles of the aerofoil, which he scratched on a silver disc now in the Science Museum, London. He went on to build a glider. At this early stage, however, his view of the possibilities of flight seems to have been limited. Of his glider, he said: 'It was very pretty to see it sail down a steep hill, and it gave the idea that a large instrument would be a better and safer conveyance down the Alps than even a sure-footed mule.' This would seem to imply that he saw flying as a sort of substitute for a funicular railway, downward bound.

Later his experiments became more lethal. He devised an internal combustion engine that ran on gunpowder, jerking forward in a series of mighty detonations that were judged a danger to life and limb. In addition, he had a full-sized glider constructed. His coachman refused point-blank to have anything to do with this engine, so Cayley prevailed upon a ten-year-old bystander to do the job. This youth soared down the side of a hill, trembling uncontrollably, some fifty years before the daylight appeared under the Wright Brothers' bootsoles at Kitty Hawk.

After his death, Cayley's ideas were eagerly snapped up by the pioneers of flight in France as well as England and were unquestionably essential to all subsequent aviation research. But somehow his name disappeared in the process, and others took the credit for his discoveries. He had been convinced that 'an uninterrupted and

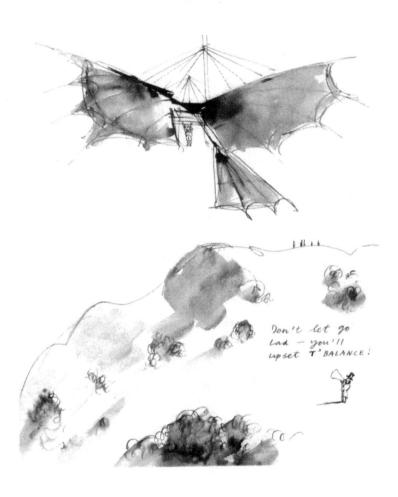

navigable ocean, that comes to the threshold of every man's door, ought not to be neglected as a source of human gratification and advantage'. The fact that we now navigate this ocean as a matter of course is largely thanks to Cayley.

Peter Chamberlen

Man-midwife by appointment

Peter Chamberlen and his descendants were responsible for the shape of English history for two hundred years. Yet in 1598, when Peter Chamberlen came to London, he was jailed after a disagreement with the Company of Barber-Surgeons.

Albert Schweitzer and Louis Pasteur have given us the idea that doctors and surgeons are motivated by compassion. Peter Chamberlen was living proof that a good proportion of them prefer money, by the sackful if possible. The Barber-Surgeons' chief complaint was that he was dishing out medicines (which surgeons were not then allowed to do) and that the medicines were not the right ones anyway. They actually had him clapped in Newgate Jail for malpractice. But by this time he already had a reputation among the fashionable, and was able to appeal to Queen Elizabeth for his release.

Soon he began to specialize in midwifery. So skilled was he that he is said to have delivered Charles I, and on the death of James I, became man-midwife to Henrietta Maria, Charles I's wife – once assisting at a stillbirth so gruesome that the Greenwich midwife, who had the first try, had passed out on the job.

Chamberlen's brilliance at difficult childbeds soon began to excite as much comment as his enormous wealth. It was observed that when he arrived at a case, he was always dressed in a long black cloak, and that he never opened his instrument bag in public. Furthermore, he always insisted that the room be cleared of spectators and other midwives before he went into action.

On Peter Chamberlen's death in 1631, his son, nephew and nephew's son succeeded to the practice. They also showed an astounding success rate at the childbed, and shared old Peter's taste for money and secretiveness. Another generation of Chamberlens followed in their footsteps, attaining extreme wealth and fame by the same means. At this point the line ended in the person of a hard-drinking satirist more interested in the first than the last moments of gestation. It was not until 1812 that the secret Peter Chamberlen had passed on to his family was revealed.

Behind a secret panel in the Chamberlen mansion was found a box, containing, among other items, four sets of obstetrical forceps. Forceps did not come into general use until the mid-eighteenth century. Before that time, the only way of making a forceps delivery (if you couldn't afford the Chamberlens) was to pull the baby out bit by bit with an instrument normally used for extracting bladder stones via the urethra. This was not good for either mother or child. Chamberlen's invention had two curved blades, to fit the baby's head, and could be taken apart so that one blade could be inserted at a time. The design is still used.

For 150 years, the Chamberlens (who would have fitted nicely into present-day Harley Street) had kept the invention to themselves. Somebody once naively asked one of them why they didn't publish their discovery far and wide, thereby reducing the sum of human suffering at a stroke. The Chamberlen replied: 'The draper is not bound to find cloth for all the naked because he hath enough in his shop, nor yet to afford it at the buyer's price.' Sound reasoning.

Among those hauled into the world by the Chamberlens were numberless nobles and several kings and queens. Charles I, Charles II, James II, Mary (wife of William of Orange) and Queen Anne spring immediately to mind. Had James I's Queen Anne not receive Chamberlen's assistance, there would have been no daughter to wed the Elector of Hanover, which might have meant no Georges. . . . It is to the Chamberlens that we owe the history of the English monarchy since 1600.

Channa

Who drove Siddartha to distraction

The chauffeurs of the mighty have caused a lot of history in their time. In pre-chauffeur times, charioteers fulfilled that function.

Channa was born and brought up on the southern borders of Nepal during the sixth century BC. In the fullness of time he secured employment as charioteer and gentleman's gentleman to a member of the local ruling family. One day, when the boss was twenty-nine years old, Channa took him for a run in the country. On their tour, they saw a bent old man.

'What is the matter with that man?' said the Prince, who had led a sheltered life.

'All men come to old age, if they live long enough,' said Channa sagely.

Next day, they went for another drive. This time they saw a sick man staggering along the verge, dressed in filthy garments.

'What is the matter with that man?' said the Prince.

'Sickness and pain are the lot of all mankind,' said Channa sagely.

Next day, on yet another drive, they saw a dead man.

'What is the matter with that man?' said the Prince.

'We all die one day,' said Channa sagely.

The Prince, who had been looking increasingly thoughtful, proposed yet another drive the following day. This time they came across a man wearing a saffron robe and a look of great serenity. On his return home the Prince was informed that his wife had borne him a son. These two events, added to Channa's answers to his questions, combined in some inscrutable manner to persuade the Prince to leave home and seek enlightenment.

Channa packed the bags and they left. The Prince announced that he was changing his name from Siddartha to Gautama. He then gave

Channa all his ornaments and costly trappings, and sent him back to the palace. It is not known what happened to Channa after this. Prince Siddartha, a.k.a. Gautama, went on to become the Buddha.

Thomas Davies

Mr Boswell—Dr Johnson, Dr Johnson— Mr Boswell

The founder of history's most famous literary partnership was the eminently ignorable Thomas Davies, a Scotsman. He was educated at Edinburgh University, and then came south to London, where he established a reputation for learning, set up as a bookseller, failed, and became an actor.

His acting career was less successful than he had hoped. In Edinburgh, he was accused of hogging the popular parts and then making a mess of them. In London, a critic accused him of 'mouthing a sentence as a dog mouths a bone', and went on to say that the only good point he could find in him was the fact that his wife was extremely pretty. This was too much to bear, and he retired from the stage forthwith.

By 1762 he set up again as a bookseller in Covent Garden. On 16 May a young Scotsman friend of his, James Boswell, chanced by as the already famous Dr Johnson was taking tea in the back parlour. Boswell begged an introduction and Davies provided it. That night, Boswell made the first Johnson entry in his journal.

Without Davies, Boswell could quite conceivably have never met Johnson. All we know of the great lexicographer would have been based on his own writings, which are frankly pretty tedious, and his other biographers, who are not only extremely tedious but inaccurate as well.

Edwin Laurentine Drake

Great bores of our time

The history of oil is long and serendipitous. Major advances seem almost invariably to have been made by otherwise insignificant characters, like Samuel Keir, the quack doctor and snake-oil salesman who invented gasoline by accident. But no character is more insignificant yet more vital than Edwin Laurentine Drake.

He was born in 1819, worked as a farm labourer, and then bettered himself by becoming a clerk. After that he became a conductor on the New York and New Haven railroad. Apparently finding this too exciting, he retired. In retirement he bought a little stock in an oil company, which like most oil companies at this time was scraping the stuff off the surface, or digging shallow trenches, near Oil Creek, Pa. Not much oil was turning up, and the company was in trouble.

One day Drake went to Oil Creek to review some title deeds. On the way he stopped off to look at some salt mines in Syracuse and Pittsburgh. Here, large drills were making boreholes, down which water was poured to dissolve the salt; the brine was then pumped back to the surface. Seized by an inspiration, Drake borrowed some equipment, rushed to Watson's Flat, Pennsylvania, and drilled the first real oil well. The modern petroleum industry had come into being.

He formed his own oil company, speculated in the oil market, and went broke. His health destroyed, he moved first to Vermont and then to Bethlehem, Pa., where he died in great poverty on 8 November 1880.

Jean-Baptiste Drouet

The man who shopped the King

The small town of Sainte-Ménéhould, in the Argonne, is famous as the birthplace of Dom Perignon, the heroic monk who put the fizz into champagne. It is also notable for the exquisite savour of its pigs' trotters and the regicidal tendencies of one of its eighteenth-century postmasters, Jean-Baptiste Drouet.

Until 1791, Drouet's life had been uneventful. He had completed his military service and settled down to an even, if discontented existence as a village functionary. Then, on 21 June 1791, a carriage changed horses in front of his post office. In the carriage was a posse of gentry – the Baroness von Korff, her two children, the children's governess and the Baroness's steward. Drouet had been stirred by the recent revolutionary disturbances in Paris. He had also seen the Queen of France a couple of times during his military service. The children looked oddly like her. And, now he came to think of it, the steward had a familiar air as well. Drouet checked the face against an *assignat* bearing the royal seal. It looked to Drouet very much as if the 'steward' was the King; which made the 'governess' (at whom he at last got a proper look) Marie Antoinette, the children the Dauphin and his sister, and the 'Baroness' the Duchess of Tourzel.

Drouet told his wife. His wife told him not to be an idiot. The carriage completed its change of horses and rolled away down the road to Varennes. A few minutes later a letter arrived for Drouet, from a Captain Bayonne. The King had escaped Paris; he was to be apprehended. Sneering briefly at his wife, Drouet mounted and rode by a back road to Varennes, where he made sure the occupants of the carriage were arrested. Three days later, they were returned to Paris and the judgement of the mob.

Drouet turned down a reward of 30,000 francs, maintaining that virtue, in this case, was its own reward. He was elected to the Convention then governing France, and became notorious for his consistently bloodthirsty line – among other things, he argued strenuously for the execution of all English residents. During the Terror, however, he urged moderation. He then espoused socialism, and was forced to flee France in 1796 after he was apprehended plotting revolution against the Revolution. From then on he was exiled, returned and was re-exiled with monotonous regularity. He died near Macon in 1824, under a false name.

Joseph Duveen

The decoy nude

Most of the great picture collections of America were effectively founded by a nude female model who sat for the French nineteenth-century painter, Bouguereau.

At the turn of the century, the millionaires of America were already showing a marked tendency to spend their spare cash on pictures. To begin with, these were not Old Masters but nineteenth-century 'story pictures' or works of the French Barbizon school – of whom Corot and Millais are the only ones still famous.

As one might expect, these pictures represented chocolate-box art at its worst. Joseph Duveen was a dealer determined to put things right and make himself millions of dollars in the process. Duveen had the grand manner, a silver tongue and a cellar full of Old Masters in which he was finding it hard to interest the chocolate-box-loving plutocrats. He was saved by a Nude by Bouguereau.

Bouguereau is no longer rated as a painter. Duveen was among the first not to rate him; but he made an exception in the case of the Nude, a voluptuous one, painted with loving modelling in eye-catchingly realistic colours. Fans of the chocolate-box could not resist the Nude. But for some reason after a while she invariably started to cloy, and Duveen invariably chose that moment to point out that a little Botticelli would be just as nice but less, well, *vulgar*. Though perhaps a bit more *expensive*. He would of course be happy to take the Nude back, at cost.

The Decoy Nude netted Duveen innumerable superior punters, many of whom he inveigled into expending their lives and fortunes in the pursuit of the pictures in which he dealt. Chief beneficiary of this was the National Gallery in Washington (itself inspired by Duveen, via the financier Mellon), filled with paintings presented by mag-

35

nates in lieu of tax. And it is fair to say that a good third of the contents of the gallery was levered in there by the brighter-than-life flesh tones and hyper-real bum of the Bouguereau Nude.

William Webb Ellis

The first scrum half

Few sportsmen have invented a national game at such a tender age as William Webb Ellis, seventeen in the year 1823.

Ellis' moment of glory came when he was playing football in the grounds of his school. The game was then in a primitive state. Devices such as cutting weapons had fallen out of favour, but teams might still contain forty or fifty players. There were still no formal rules – except that the game was to be played with the feet, not the hands. Picking up the ball and running with it was frowned on. There was no referee to blow the whistle on the runner, but pressure of popular opinion, backed up by boots, made it inadvisable.

Apparently this did not bother William Webb Ellis, who was not only indifferent to public opinion but big for his age. A member of the opposing team kicked the ball high in the air, and he caught it. So far so good. Catching was legal. After a catch, the catcher was entitled to a free kick, while the opposing team was not allowed to come beyond the site of the catch until the ball had touched the ground or been kicked by the catcher. William Webb Ellis did not have time for all this rigmarole. He took a furtive look round, and began running, ball in hand, across Bigside at Rugby, straight for the opposing goal. Rugby Football had been born.

It is not known whether or not he scored. In the words of the Rugby magazine, 'it was an act which if a fag had ventured to have done, he would probably have received more kicks than commendation.' But William Webb Ellis was no fag.

On leaving Rugby, Ellis continued to buck the odds. At Oxford he took Holy Orders, becoming particularly interested in the conversion of Jews to Christianity. He wrote several books with this in mind, but they made little mark on his prospective converts or posterity.

His historical importance is not merely to Rugby Football. Certainly without him the Rugby code would in all probability never have developed. But then nor would the Football Association, founded as it was in the heresies and faction fighting between the different codes. William Webb Ellis not only started the glory that is Twickenham and Cardiff Arms Park; he is equally responsible for the Cup Final.

Farinelli

Crooner by appointment, and keeper of the peace

The eminent male soprano and saviour of the kings of Spain, Farinelli, was born in 1705 under the name of Carlo Broschi, and was shortly afterwards castrated. He was trained under the patronage of the Neapolitan family of the Farinas – and presumably changed his name in favour of them.

It rapidly became clear that Farinelli was an exceptionally talented songster. At an early age he won a fast-high-note-producing competition against a trumpeter, and was soon singing lead parts in opera both in his native Italy and abroad. During a visit to England, he sang in the same production as Seresino, one of his principal rivals. Seresino was playing an elderly tyrant, and Farinelli the youthful hero who had fallen into his power. So affecting was the first aria of Farinelli that Seresino, charmed out of character, rushed across the stage and embraced him in an ecstasy of remorseful compassion.

But it is more for his private than his public triumphs that the Apulian Nightingale deserves to be remembered. At the age of thirty-two he went to Spain where King Philip V had gone melancholy mad. The King's gloom was not incomprehensible, because the English had recently stolen Gibraltar from him, and an alliance of French, Dutch and English had urged an alternative king of Spain. It was generally felt, however, that the monarch had gone over the top even by the standard of Spanish kings. He no longer shaved or cut his hair or fingernails, seldom if ever changed his clothes, and for reasons best known to himself had transposed day and night so that audiences scheduled for say 2 p.m. were actually held at 2 a.m. The haggard courtiers asked Farinelli if he would sing for the King, in the hope of cheering him up. Farinelli obliged. The results were startling.

After four songs, the King demanded barber and manicurist, and after a spring-cleaning once again grasped the reins of state. Farinelli sang him those same four songs every night for the next ten years, keeping him in the best of mental health and in the process becoming an important – if not the most important – figure in the Spanish court. Farinelli was co-opted by the anti-French lobby, and was able to fill Philip's ear with useful propaganda as well as songs. The rather supine monarch was thus stiffened to resist the overtures of the rest of Europe. Farinelli beguiled the hours between audiences by reforming the music of the royal chapel and building a new opera house. Less conventionally, he also took to importing Hungarian horses and devised an ambitious scheme for the diversion of the river Tagus.

On the death of Philip V, his successor Ferdinand VI kept Farinelli on as royal soother. His reign was one of the calmest and most pacific Spain has ever experienced, largely as a result of the Nightingale's ministrations. On Ferdinand's death and the accession of Charles III, Farinelli retired to Bologna in Italy, where he lived to a distinguished old age.

Thomas Farriner

The baker who demolished London

Little is known of the early years of Thomas Farriner, who, with a simple bread oven, changed the face of London in five days more than Richard Seifert and his computerized draughtsmen in ten years.

It is recorded that, having undergone an apprenticeship, he set up as a master baker. It is likewise recorded that his produce was extremely toothsome, and won him the custom of no less a personage than Charles II. His house and bakery were in Pudding Lane, one of the reeking thoroughfares typical of London in the year after the Great Plague. Here he lived in reasonable felicity with two servants and his daughter Harriet.

On Saturday, 2 September 1666, Farriner was awakened by the screams of his maid. It was 2 a.m. and she was being burned to death. Farriner and Harriet escaped, and watched from the street as the fire spread to the neighbouring houses. At 3 a.m. they were joined by the Lord Mayor, Sir Thomas Bludworth, summoned by reports of a hellish conflagration. Bludworth was not impressed. 'Pish!' he said. 'A woman might piss it out.' Having delivered this line, he returned to bed.

As it happened, the combined efforts of the inhabitants of London, women included, failed to extinguish the blaze. It raged till the Wednesday, destroying most of the buildings within the city walls.

Farriner was by this time telling anyone who would listen that it couldn't have been his fault. He had gone round at midnight, and there had been no fires lit except in one room, where the floor had been paved with brick, and he had personally (as a skilled baker of long standing) raked the ashes up into an entirely accident-proof pile. It was, he maintained, a clear-cut case of arson.

And, immediately after the fire, an arsonist was discovered –

LONDON
As it could have been.

Soho
↓

Knightsbridge
↓

42

Sloane Square ↓

Chigwell →

Old
Mother Thames

John
Glashan

Robert Hubert, who admitted throwing a fireball in at Farriner's window. Actually Hubert's confession was only one of dozens, but he was hanged anyway and everyone felt better. Subsequently Londoners, including Farriner, put the fire down to the Catholics. A Frenchman insisted that he was one of 300 highly trained incendiaries who had been infiltrated into the city by his evil masters to put it to the torch. Farriner professed belief in this and all successive versions except those that involved his own carelessness. One theory he disputed with great vehemence was that his apprentice had left a bundle of twigs to dry in the oven overnight, and that they had overheated and caught fire. It may be no coincidence that this is now accepted as by far the most likely explanation.

Once the ashes had cooled, it was generally agreed that whoever started the fire deserved not the noose but a medal of some kind. Only four people died. The lingering germs of the previous year's plague were destroyed, and the ground laid bare for Wren to build the City churches, St Paul's and the elegant public and domestic buildings that still stand (except where they have been flattened by bombs or developers). Farriner's little accident happened at precisely the right moment. If the Old City had survived, it would have continued to breed pestilence. Worse, it would undoubtedly have been razed and rebuilt at a later date – and the most likely rebuilders would have been the Victorians. A Victorian St Paul's? A Gothic Cornhill? Perish the thought! Nice work, Mr Farriner!

Harry Gem

The real tennis pioneer

In the foyer of the Lawn Tennis Association in Wimbledon, there stands the bust of a forbidding gentleman called Major Walter Clopton Wingfield. The bust is labelled 'The Inventor of Lawn Tennis'. This is totally untrue. Wingfield invented a game called, bizarrely, Sphairistike, loosely based on real tennis. The inventor of lawn tennis was the utterly insignificant (though charming) Major Harry Gem.

Harry was a solicitor and clerk to the Birmingham magistrates. He and a Spanish friend, Señor J.B. Perera, began knocking a ball over a net in Perera's garden in 1859, also using a set of rules simplified from real tennis. Finding it an invigorating pursuit, they enlisted the support of a couple of local doctors and founded the world's first 'lawn tennis' club at the Manor House Hotel, Leamington Spa. The year was 1872.

It was not until two years later that Major Walter Clopton Wingfield evolved his own game. It was played on an hourglass-shaped court to an unspeakably complicated set of rules. While the good Major Gem perfected his volley in the Midlands, Clopton weaselled his way into the good graces of the LTA's tame sculptors. In tennis, then as now, the winner is sometimes the one with the biggest mouth.

F. C. Gimson

For King, country and colony

Ever since its founding by unscrupulous imperialist dope peddlers in the early nineteenth century, Hong Kong has represented a bonanza for Westerners in the East. After the Second World War, the bonanza reached astounding proportions. This is due entirely to the efforts of one man, an obscure civil servant, F.C. Gimson.

Gimson was a strong-minded individualist, the son of a Leicestershire parson. He was posted to Hong Kong in 1941. Immediately afterwards the Japanese invaded it, and interned all British civilians in Stanley barracks.

There followed nearly four years of hell, as the Japanese tortured and executed those prisoners who failed to toe their line. Gimson distinguished himself as spokesman and unofficial leader of the internees. They were cut off from news of the outside world. So when on 15 August 1945 the Japanese began to treat him with a new and startling civility, he was at first taken aback. Then, deducing that the Allies had won the war, he took it upon himself to assume command of the colony of Hong Kong.

What he did not know at the time was that, following the general carve-up of the Potsdam Conference, the Americans (ignoring the fact that it was none of their damn business) had promised Chiang Kai Shek, the Chinese supremo, that he could have Hong Kong back. This fact Gimson managed to deduce from the general shiftiness of the Chinese and the defeated Japanese, as well as the information that finally began to filter through from the British Government. He therefore assumed the title of Lieutenant Governor, an *ad hoc* invention, and managed to hang on by the skin of his teeth until the British Fleet arrived some weeks later.

But for Gimson, the most prosperous years of Hong Kong's life would have vanished – first under the occupation of the Nationalist Chinese and subsequently under the Communists.

John Gough

Who knew what the matter was

Einstein, Planck, Hiroshima and Bikini Atoll might today never have been heard of had it not been for Blind John Gough.

He was born in the Lake District in 1757. Smallpox left him blind at the age of two, but he had already developed the unstoppable curiosity that was to characterize his every move in later life. He began studying plants by touch, fingering their stalks and leaves and licking their pistils and stamens. The finest hairs he detected with his lower lip. His studies advanced so rapidly that before the age of fifteen he was conducting a botany class attended by his schoolmates.

Gough had a remarkable memory, which enabled him to quote at length from Greek, Latin and English poets after very few hearings. As well as the Classics, he studied physics. His gifts excited the admiration of Samuel Taylor Coleridge, who wrote: 'The every way amiable and estimable John Gough of Kendal is not only an excellent mathematician, but an infallible botanist and zoologist . . . the rapidity of his touch appears fully equal to that of sight, and the accuracy greater.'

He published work on (among other topics) suspended animation in vegetables, the Ebbing Well at Giggleswick (Yorks.), scoteography, or writing in the dark, the effacement of lakes, and – most importantly for posterity – the Mixture of Gases. Soon afterwards he turned to mathematics using an abacus of his own design and taking as a pupil John Dalton, who was a Cumberland Quaker like him.

Dalton turned out to have one of the foremost scientific minds of the age. It is said to be as a direct result of his fortuitous meeting with Gough and Gough's work on the Mixture of Gases that Dalton arrived at the conclusion, delivered in a series of lectures to his Royal

Institution in 1803-4, that matter was composed of groups of tiny particles, called atoms. On this discovery rests all subsequent work on the Atomic Theory.

Lisa Gioconda

Smile, please!

One of the most famous Small Parts was born in Naples in about 1480, and in the last years of the century became the second or third wife of a Mr Zenobio Giocondo of Florence. Mr Giocondo, perhaps conscious through past experience of the impermanence of wives and wishing for a keepsake, arranged for her portrait to be painted. This was done between 1503 and 1506, the sitter being entertained not only by the fascinating chatter of the artist, Leonardo da Vinci, but also by musicians hired for her diversion. For either or both of these reasons she spent much of these three years smiling a smile which some have described as placid, and others mysterious.

The finished portrait is known to foreigners as *La Gioconda*, and to English speakers as the *Mona Lisa*, a mispelling of Monna (short for Madonna) Lisa, the lady's first name.

I like it, but there's something wrong with the mouth ...

Father Grandet

The priest who rescued the province

The French in the seventeenth century were as keen on torture as the rest of Europe, if not keener. The one thing they considered outrageously cruel – then as now – was being forced to eat bad food.

This fact was brilliantly exploited by Father Grandet, director of the seminary at Angers, during the fearful Anjou famine of 1683. The countryside was full of starving peasants after the harvest had failed. Charitably, Grandet first of all forced each bourgeois family in the towns to adopt and feed a peasant family. Next, he filled carts with bread and sent them into the countryside. But there were too few bourgeois families to go round, and hordes of peasants, faces blackened with famine, attacked the bread carts as soon as they left the city gates. Grandet appealed repeatedly to the King, but no help came.

The last resort of the starving was a sort of greenish bread made from the leaves of ferns. Grandet had the inspiration of sending a sample loaf to Versailles. It created a sensation. Amazed and horrified courtiers flocked to gaze on it. The King broke off a piece, nibbled and spat. Famine was one thing: but this bread was . . . well, *insupportable*.

The King ordered emergency relief. Within twenty-four hours, Anjou was awash with soup and bobbing with croutons. The famine ended there and then. Hundreds of thousands of Angevins, among them the forebears of the Douanier Rousseau and the surgeon Ambroise Paré, owed their lives to Father Grandet, who forthwith returned to the holy obscurity whence he had come.

Lord Grey de Werk

A rebellion bogged down in the Rhine

The seventeenth century in England is noted as no other for its political upheavals. No man had so great an influence on the century as the insignificant Lord Grey de Werk.

Grey was typical of his age – a smooth, hard-surfaced courtier, twisty as a Salomonic column and with the morals of an alley-cat. He achieved a certain notoriety as a Whig parliamentarian – which at the time meant that he opposed the Roman Catholicism then creeping back under the aegis of the recently restored Stuarts. This made him a friend of the Duke of Monmouth. But his principal fame, during the early part of his life, was due to his marital and extramarital adventures.

Having married Mary Berkeley, he proceeded to have an affair with her seventeen-year-old sister Henrietta. This was conducted secretly, and under difficult circumstances – on one occasion, Grey was forced to hide in Henrietta's wardrobe for two days, living only on the morsels she was from time to time able to push through the keyhole.

Soon after this, Grey was arrested as a principal in the Rye House Plot to murder Charles II. *En route* for the Tower of London, Grey and the two arresting officers paused for dinner at a tavern, where at Grey's instigation they demolished fourteen bottles of claret. On arrival at the Tower, the carriage was found to contain a stotious prisoner's escort but no prisoner, Grey having legged it for Flanders.

In Flanders, a plotting season had opened beside which all other plotting seasons paled into insignificance, spurred on by the death of Charles II and the accession of the ghastly James II. The central thrust of the plotting, and that of which Grey was chief instigator, was to land in the West Country, oust James II from the throne, and

53

install the Duke of Monmouth in his place. An Armada set sail, and arrived at Lyme Regis, Dorset, on 11 June 1685. Grey was in command of the cavalry, a role for which he was fitted chiefly by his excellent leg for a riding boot.

At Bridport, Grey's cavalry was repulsed by a terrifying force of Dorset hobbledehoys armed with pitchforks and intimidating rusty matchlocks. This was rather a shock for Monmouth, who had expected better things of his commander; but he was a tolerant man, and he allowed Grey to retain his command. The invaders marched on to Sedgemoor, and Destiny.

Sedgemoor is a flat part of Somerset, criss-crossed with deep black ditches. There was extant a prophecy that if Monmouth ever visited the Rhine, it would be his undoing. As a result of this, he had vigorously steered clear of that river. Imagine his gloom when he discovered that 'rhine' is the Sedgemoor word for 'ditch', and that thanks to Grey's plotting he now had to visit thousands of the things. His gloom deepened when Grey, at the head of the cavalry, halted at a rhine in the face of the enemy and (according to contemporary witnesses) fell in. Monmouth's infantry fired a volley. The King's infantry fired back; two of Grey's men were killed. Grey wheeled his horse and once again legged it from the field.

The rest is history. Judge Jeffreys conducted his 'bloody assizes'. Monmouth's head was hacked ineptly from his shoulders. But Grey survived – indeed, some said he had been a double agent throughout.

With William and Mary's accessions he was restored to favour, and died in 1701. They buried him in Westminster Abbey, with a pipeful of tobacco by his side.

It is men like Grey who gave the Restoration its fine reputation for callousness, debauchery, libertinism and double dealing. Had the Monmouth rebellion succeeded, it is conceivable that there would have been no William of Orange, and no ineffably tedious Hanoverians.

Sir John Harington

Gloriana and Ajax

Sir John Harington, the inventor of the water closet, is a shining example of the heights accessible to those with the right family and education. At the accession to the throne of Elizabeth I, John's parents were much in the royal favour, having virtually been cellmates with Elizabeth in the Tower of London during the bloody reign of Mary. Indeed Queen Elizabeth had agreed to be the infant John's godmother.

The youth attended Eton and Cambridge, where he began to show signs of a marked fizziness of disposition. This tendency became more pronounced at court, where he made a translation of certain naughty bits from Ariosto's *Orlando Furioso* for the Queen's ladies. The ladies loved it, but the Queen, who also took a look at it, did not. John was therefore banished to Kelston, his wife's estate near Bath. Here he undertook the programme of research works which culminated in the building of the world's first water closet.

Mechanically it was reasonably similar to modern specimens. The pan itself was an oval bucket, its floor sloping to the back and the right hand side. Water was carried from a tank in the room above, via a lead pipe, to a tap under the seat at the back. Substances made their exit from the pan via a sluice at its lowest point, controlled by a system of levers, which was lockable. Lockability was necessary because the sluice was not connected to a sewer but was designed to be emptied by a servant with a bucket; the results of tampering with the sluice by 'children or other busie persons' would set at naught the object of the device, which was the 'sweetnesse' of the house.

As well as designing the first w.c., Harington also wrote the first of the numerous books meant to be read at stool. Entitled *The Metamorphosis of Ajax*, this was a work pointing out the merits of the new system and raising merely physical acts to a metaphysical plane:

> *Pure prayer ascends to Him that high doth sit,*
> *Downe falls the filth, for fiends of hell more fit.*

Elizabeth was introduced to the device during a visit to Kelston, and was so impressed that she commissioned one for her own use in the Palace of Richmond. A copy of the *Metamorphosis* was kept chained next to it. Riding high on the success of his invention, John Harington returned to court. He was soon banished again, not this time on account of general rudeness but for giving cheek to the Earl of Leicester, Elizabeth's favourite.

In 1598, his sins partially forgotten, he was allowed to accompany the Earl of Essex on his ill-fated expedition to suppress an Irish rebellion. After the Irish expedition, Harington became famous for his liberal attitudes to Irish affairs, and in later life caused general hilarity by applying for the job of Archbishop of Ireland, on the grounds that he thought more like an Irishman than an Englishman.

After his death, his water closet, books, and general rudeness passed into silence – a silence from which they were not liberated until 1775, when a design appeared bearing powerful similarities to Harington's, and made its 'inventor' a fortune.

George Harrison

South Africa was his fault

George Harrison was a vagrant from nowhere in particular whose only claim to fame is that he endowed South Africa with its present enormous wealth. He was nominally a prospector, and under this pretext had shuffled across most of Australia and a good deal of Africa, entering history only on arrival at Witwatersrand. Here he was dragging himself across the arid plain when he chanced to kick a pebble that glittered. What the pebble glittered with was gold. The larger chunk of rock off which the pebble had broken was the Mother Lode or Main Reef, which apparently surfaced a stone's throw from where he was standing.

The magistrates declared it a Public Goldfield, and the rush began. Harrison staked a claim, No. 19, and hung about wearing a dazed expression while a town grew up around him, populated partly by Boers and partly by the scum of five continents, especially good-for-nothings from Britain. In the manner of many lucky prospectors, Harrison then sold his claim for £15, shuffled off into the sunset, and was eaten by a lion, entirely unaware that by his discovery he had changed African history rather more radically than Cecil Rhodes.

Tension between Boers and British gold-diggers was one of the causes of the Boer War. And ever since that day it is South African gold which has financed the bizarre and socially unacceptable behaviour of successive South African governments.

Robert Henderson

Unlucky striker

Robert Henderson, the son of a Nova Scotia lighthouse keeper, has the distinction of scoring one of history's most important near misses. He became a prospector at the age of fourteen. By 1896 he had worked his way round America and Canada to fetch up at the Indian River country in Canada's Northwest Territories. Here his two companions of the moment, fed up with wet feet, flapjacks and mosquitoes, left for civilization. Henderson started walking.

He did not go far. He climbed one of the tributaries of the Indian River to the watershed, and looked down on another river system, across swamp, moose-pasture and streams. It looked vaguely promising (to Henderson the next valley always looked vaguely promising). He strolled down to the creek, unshipped his pan, and tried his luck. The first pan yielded eight cents' worth of gold dust, which was better than promising. He staked a claim, named the creek Gold Bottom after the New Jerusalem that he considered lay on the bedrock, and made his way back towards the nearest trading post. *En route* he met a certain George Carmack, fishing.

Carmack was a white man who had adopted the Indian way of life. Henderson did not approve of this, but he knew his duty as a white man and a prospector (motto: *Do as you would be done by*). He told him that he had struck gold. He added, with a nod at Carmack's Indian companions, that he didn't want any of them Siwashes staking up there. Carmack, loyal to his Indian friends, observed that it was a big country and that he'd find a creek of his own. They parted ways.

A few days later, Henderson was working at Gold Bottom when Carmack strolled up and told him he had staked a claim over the ridge at Rabbit Creek. His Siwash companions tried to buy tobacco off Henderson, who sent them packing. Carmack said that he'd send word if his claim produced anything worthwhile and disappeared. Some weeks afterwards, rumours reached Henderson of a rich strike at a place called Bonanza, which he recognized as the former Rabbit Creek. Carmack had made the first strike, and claims were now staked as far as the eye could see.

Henderson's less than tolerant attitude to the Indians had presumably caused Carmack to 'forget' his promised tip-off, and thus to miss getting in on the ground floor of what within six months had become the Klondike Gold Rush.

He headed back to town, staking various claims on the way. But when he reached the land office, he found that the rules had changed and he was able to register only one claim. Protesting bitterly, he registered the Gold Bottom claim and set off downriver towards his wife and family, whom he had not seen for four years.

Gold Bottom, though not prime Klondike like Bonanza, eventually produced about a million dollars. But this did Henderson no good, because he had fallen ill in an icebound river steamer at Circle City, and had sold his claim for $3000 to pay his medical bills.

He spent the remainder of his life prospecting in Canada and Alaska, and died of cancer in 1933.

Johann Georg Hiedler

The naughty miller repents

Wandering millers have always comprised a suspect class of person, but you would have to go a long way before you found one with as much to answer for as a Mr Johann Georg Hiedler, of Lower Austria.

In 1842, Johann married Maria Anna Schicklgruber. Five years previously, Maria had given birth to a son, Alois, out of wedlock. In 1847, Maria died and Johann, bereft of cook and housekeeper, went for a thirty-year stroll. But in 1877 he reappeared, and swore before notaries that Maria's illegitimate son Alois had been sired by him, Johann.

The notary forthwith wrote to the priest of the church where Alois' birth had been registered, instructing him to change the particulars in the register. No longer should the entry occur under the name Shicklgruber. Instead, the name should be Hiedler (spelt a new, updated way, thus: Hitler). In time, Alois Hitler (né Shicklgruber) sired a son, Adolf. And that very Adolf was heard in later life to speculate that had his grandfather the miller not sworn his oath before the notary and changed the name, matters might have developed differently.

Try it. Raising the right arm stiffly from the shoulder, fill the facial veins with blood and howl (imagining 20,000 of like mind at your back, among the flickering torches of Nuremberg):

HEIL SHICKLGRUBER!

No, it just wouldn't have caught on. Johann and his notary caused WWII, sure as shooting.

John Howard

Fleeing newshound saves nation drama

It seems unlikely that John Howard, an English colliery manager living in the middle of nowhere some seventy-five miles from Pretoria, South Africa, ever saw himself as a political kingmaker. By all accounts he led a reasonably humdrum life, managing a workmanlike colliery and minding his own business. Then, on 13 December 1899, as he was preparing for a lonely expatriate Christmas, there was a knock on his door. No doubt Howard was rather perturbed, since the countryside was at that time infested with revolting Boers. But he opened the door, and in marched History.

It appeared in the person of a journalist who had recently escaped from a Boer POW camp, in which he had been immured for showing a readiness to shoot as well as write. He had been on the run for some days and was extremely tired, having been gnawed by rats while hiding down a mineshaft, and eyed up by vultures while lying doggo in a wood. His name was Winston Churchill; nobody at that time had ever heard of him.

Howard looked after Churchill for the best part of a week, then disguised him as a bale of wool and loaded him on a train for Lourenço Marques, beyond the war zone. From there he made his way to Durban. His account of his adventures was extremely exciting (and managed to ignore the fact that the Boers had planned to release him the morning following his escape). In fact it was so exciting that he achieved international fame. From that moment, he never looked back.

Had Howard not given him the chance to complete his clandestine journey, Churchill would have had nothing to write about. He might have gone from story to story, winding up as an exhausted hack accepting charity and claret in a corner of El Vino's.

62

Henry Hunt

The riotous assemblyman

Henry Hunt is one of the spiritual forebears of the Speaker's Corner soapbox artistes – except that if you listened to Henry, you could wind up dead.

Hunt's background gave no cause to suspect the flood of rhetoric that lay in store. He was born in 1773 into a prosperous Wiltshire farming family. Admittedly he was a delicate child, which is sometimes a bad sign. But the first sign that something was wrong was when he ran away from school on the grounds that the schoolmaster was cruel – akin, in the late eighteenth century, to running away from water on the grounds that it is wet.

His father wanted him to go into the church, but luckily for the church he had other ideas – the first of which was to enlist as a clerk on a slave-ship. His father dissuaded him, and then gave evidence of his remarkable rhetorical powers by describing a local barmaid in such glowing terms that Henry fell in love with her sight unseen, hijacked her and married her.

There followed a few comparitively normal years. As a part-time soldier in the Yeomanry, Henry found himself perfectly in sympathy with military ideals. Bonaparte was a bad thing, and England a good one. After the war, however, Henry became mixed up with radicals like the splendid William Cobbett. His work, as he now saw it, lay in the cause of Reform, and he proved a talented orator, or (in the words of Radical colleagues as well as political opponents) an 'unprincipled demagogue'.

The climax of his career occurred on 16 August 1819, in Manchester, where he was speaking to a large but orderly crowd which had assembled to hear him at St Peter's Fields. Local magistrates, overreacting to Hunt's reputation as a rabble-rouser, ordered the

Yeomanry to open fire, entirely neglecting the fact that the rabble was unroused. Eleven people (including women and children) were killed, and 400 injured. Henry himself was unhurt. On his release from jail he managed (after some trouble) to get elected to Parliament, where he made a nuisance of himself for a couple of years, alienating his old allies the Radicals as well as the government. Flung out by his constituents in 1833, he devoted the remaining two years of his life to the manufacture of boot polish.

The Peterloo Massacre, which might not have happened if Hunt had not chosen to address the crowds that day, marked the lowest point in the civil unrest that followed the Napoleonic Wars. It is fair to say that the breach between the common people and the authorities became institutionalized as from that day. The Six Acts, passed as a direct response to the Peterloo Massacre, provided for censorship, tight arms control, speedy administration of justice, and the suppression or control of demonstrations. In spite of their savage repressiveness and unjust origins (for instance, the crowd at Peterloo was not armed) the Six Acts, much modified, remain the foundation for legislation in these areas today.

Dr William Hunter

The tale of the sharper younger brother

In his day, Dr William Hunter would have been astonished if anyone had accused him of insignificance. He was at the head of his profession and famous throughout Britain. Unfortunately his fame has not persisted – except in one rather curious detail.

He was born in Scotland in 1717, and joined the perennial migration of Scottish doctors to London. By 1748 he was lecturing in surgery and anatomy (though his kindly disposition made him a poor practising surgeon in those grisly pre-anaesthetic days). At about this time his mother wrote him a plaintive letter from Scotland. His youngest brother John, a spoilt brat who had refused to learn to read and had as a result been apprenticed to an Edinburgh cabinet-maker, had just got the sack. Could he do anything to help?

The kindly Hunter sent for his brother, who arrived with his tool kit and was soon hard at work among the cadavers. In fact he showed such an aptitude for dissection that William gave him a job as demonstrator. From then on there was no stopping him. While William plodded away, John broke new ground. William went over old ground in lymphatics; John evolved the foundations of scientific surgery. William wrote on the 'Uncertainty of the Signs of Murder in the Case of Bastard Children'; John wrote a 'Treatise on the Natural History of the Human Teeth', which laid the foundations for modern dentistry. William wrote about the Nyl-ghau, an obscure type of Indian antelope; John was the teacher and lifelong friend of Jenner, who invented vaccination and rid the world of smallpox. (Indeed, he was one of the earliest guinea-pigs. When he died it is said to have been as a result of an experimental self-inoculation.)

Towards the end of their lives William and John fell out, possibly because William was by now attempting to pass off John's work as

his own. Whatever the truth of the matter, the fact remains that it is the insignificant William, whose contribution to modern medicine is negligible, who is the more important of the two. Had he not given John and his woodworking tools a shot at the corpses, nobody would ever have heard of him. Or, for that matter, of decent dentistry, scientific surgery or vaccination.

Major F.G. Jackson

The man who blighted Robert Falcon Scott

Major F.G. Jackson was a superb specimen of the type of Englishman, insensitive to extremes of temperature, who regarded the Empire as his back garden and spent a good deal of time strolling to and fro in its less hospitable bits. While he led a useful life, he deserves notice chiefly because he made it possible for Amundsen to reach the South Pole in 1911.

Jackson was born in Worcestershire in 1860. By the time he was thirty-two, he had travelled extensively in the Australian outback, and made a sledge journey across the great tundra of Siberia. In 1894 he led an expedition to the North Pole. When it became evident that the expedition was not going to achieve its objective, he spent three years exploring Franz Josef Land. It was hereabouts in June 1896 that he marched resolutely into immortality.

In 1894, the Norwegian explorer Fridtjof Nansen had been in the process of trying to drift round the North of Russia, locked in the ice in his ship *Fram*. Becoming bored with the literally glacier-like slowness of the drift, he had left the ship and walked towards the North Pole. On returning, he was appalled to discover that the *Fram* had moved, and was nowhere to be seen. He spent an uncomfortable winter on the icecap with one companion, and the following summer had managed to walk as far as Franz Josef Land before his food and strength ran out. As he reached the frozen shore, the brave Nansen emitted despairing Nordic howls. All, it appeared, was lost. But his howls were heard by Jackson, who chanced to be behind a rock just down the coast, and the Nansen team were rescued forthwith.

Without Jackson, Nansen would certainly have perished. Without Nansen, the *doyen* of polar exploration at the turn of the century, Amundsen would almost certainly have been inadequately equipped for his South Polar bid – not least because it was the *Fram* that carried his party to Antarctica. Without Amundsen Captain Scott would have been the first man to reach the South Pole.

Captain Robert Jenkins

The man with the pickled ear

The notoriety of Captain Robert Jenkins stems from his ear, the only one on record as having caused a major war. The origins of this remarkable figure are unhappily shrouded in mystery, as is his entire life until he sailed into the viewfinder of History on board the ship *Rebecca*, carrying sugar from Jamaica to London in 1731. On 9 April they had the misfortune to come across the notorious Captain Fandino, a Spaniard of amazing touchiness. Fandino accused Jenkins of looting Spanish colonies. When he denied this charge, the Spaniard first hacked up a mulatto cabin-boy. He then tied Jenkins' wrists behind his back, ran him up to the foreyard, and jerked him about a bit in an attempt to persuade him to reveal where he had stashed his treasure. Jenkins, a tough egg, held his peace. Fandino then chopped off his ear and advised him to take it to King George, pillaged the *Rebecca* and sailed about his business.

Jenkins sailed home to London, leaving the severed ear to steep in a jar of rum. On arrival he took it to the King, who promised to do something about it, presumably in order to get rid of Jenkins who must have been no oil painting. It was not until 1739, seven years later when Jenkins had more or less forgotten the whole incident, that he was summoned before a Commons Trading Committee, investigating quarrels with Spain. The bottled ear was waved about to tremendous effect and caused the mob to howl for Spanish blood. War was declared on Spain and its ally, France. A fleet was sent to Porto Bello, the gold capital of Central America, under the command of Admiral 'Old Grog' Vernon. In 1740 it merged imperceptibly with the War of the Austrian Succession, and hostilities did not end till 1748.

Charles Jennens

Who lent a hand to Handel

It must be extremely irritating when you have written half of one of the musical masterpieces of the English language, to have a German come and swipe all the credit. This was the unfortunate lot of Charles Jennens, (born 1700) otherwise known as Solyman the Magnificent, an extremely rich person of Gopsall, Leicestershire.

In his town house on Great Ormond Street, he dabbled in the arts, surrounded by yes-men. His principal achievement in early life was to publish what he claimed was a definitive edition of Shakespeare. In this he combined typographical errors from earlier editions with new ones of his own. The critics, amongst whom was Dr Johnson, were not amused. But Jennens did not let this worry him. For one thing, he was rich enough to rise above the squibs of Grub Street. For another, he had met a composer called Handel, and Handel was writing some pretty fair accompaniments to lyrics by Jennens. Some of them were all right, anyway. Others did not, in Jennens' opinion, measure up. There was one in particular that Handel introduced without so much as a by your leave, on the grounds that the ending of Jennens' *Saul* was insufficiently grand. This tune was the 'Hallelujah Chorus', which in Handel's opinion injected exactly the right amount of grandness into the part that lacked it. Jennens was miffed. 'If [the conclusion were not Grand enough] it was [Handel's] own fault,' he wrote, 'for the words would have bore as Grand Musick as he could have set 'em: but this Hallelujah, Grand as it is, comes in very nonsensically.' Handel's head, he concluded, was full of maggots.

Jennens wrote *Israel in Egypt* as well as *Saul* and the *Messiah*. But it is the *Messiah* for which he is remembered, or rather *not* remembered. The notices in Ireland, where it received its first favourable reviews, spoke of 'the most elevated, majestick and moving words'. Jennens, a man of strongly individual opinions, nevertheless considered that Handel could have done better, given the quality of the libretto.

Raymond Jones

The Beat Brothers fan

The early career of Raymond Jones showed no sign that he was going to change the listening habits of a generation. He was born in 1943, and by 1961 was a printer's apprentice, living in Huyton, Liverpool. At weekends he liked to go to the odd dance. On 27 October 1961, he landed up at his regular Friday night spot, Hambledon Hall.

Jones was really a Carl Perkins fan, but his tastes were catholic. On this Friday night the DJ Bob Wooler played a record made by a local group in Germany and advised the revellers to get down to their record retailers and demand it forthwith.

As it happened, Jones worked just down the road from NEMS, a shop that advertised 'The Finest Record Collection in the North'. Jones was a regular customer here, partly because the manager had a policy of getting any record asked for, no matter how obscure.

That Saturday, the manager himself was serving behind the counter, helping out with the weekend rush. By chance it was him that Jones asked for his record. The manager had never heard of the group. Their name had to be spelled out for him. It was Beatles, with an 'a'. As far as Jones could remember, the label of the record was foreign. The manager, whose name was Epstein, wrote on his notepad: 'The Beatles – check Monday'.

The record Jones had been seeking was 'My Bonnie', sung by the Beatles under the *nom de guerre* of Tony Sheridan and the Beat Brothers, but announced by the disc jockey as being by the Beatles. It is said to have been a big disappointment to Jones. But Epstein had been obliged to visit a lunchtime session at the Cavern Club, in order to find out about the record from one George Harrison, an erstwhile Beat Brother. What he saw and heard led him to become the group's manager.

Raymond Jones, who had brought about that introduction, stepped modestly out of public life.

Friedrich Kasiski

The codebreaker who shot Germany in the foot

The life of Friedrich Kasiski was one of unparalleled monotony. He was born in 1805 in the town of Schlochau in West Prussia – a flat spot, without redeeming features or indeed features of any kind at all. At the age of seventeen Kasiski joined the East Prussian 33rd Infantry Regiment. After three years, he was commissioned second lieutenant, a rank which he held for fourteen tedious years until 1839. Promotion then accelerated a little and by the time he retired in 1852 he held the rank of major.

After his retirement, this grey non-eminence devoted himself for a few years to the training of a Territorial Army regiment, and to fiddling about with codes and ciphers. The product of his scratchings was a book with the title of *Die Geheimschriften und die Dechiffrirkunst* – 'Ciphers and How to Crack Them'. It dealt exclusively with the mind-boggling complexities of solving polyalphabetic ciphers with repeating keywords, and was received in a deafening critical silence. Kasiski seems not to have cared as he had found a new hobby – digging up Bronze Age mounds near Danzig. He died in 1881.

It was well after his death that his importance became evident. In the *Dechiffrirkunst*, Kasiski reveals himself as a stout patriot by including a chapter on French, presumably in preparation for the Franco-Prussian War. He would have been depressed to know that some thirty-six years later, in the very secret Room 40 at the Admiralty in London, the methods described in his book were among those used by the cryptanalysts de Grey and Montgomery to arrive at the plaintext of the Zimmerman telegram. For it was the Zimmerman telegram, proposing an alliance between Germany and Mexico against the USA, that brought the USA into the First World War thus ensuring Germany's defeat.

Madame Kleinmuller

Napoleon's Nemesis

History is full of soothsayers. But few of them have demonstrated as little regard for the sooth as Madame Kleinmuller, who killed Napoleon Bonaparte.

Kleinmuller's life story is obscure. The only certain sightings were in Rome around the year 1820. Here she swept about the streets draped in black merino, with an Empire-style turban from beneath which her eyes flashed alarmingly. Rome at this time was as full of spies as it is now full of Fiats; it is therefore not surprising that she is said to have combined her fortune-telling with a little light eavesdropping on behalf of Metternich.

In Rome she wormed her way into the good graces of Marie-Letizia, the mother of Napoleon, who was not unnaturally worried about her son, captive on faraway St Helena. Her worry was in no way allayed when Kleinmuller informed her that in a dream she had seen Napoleon being removed from St Helena by angels, and taken to a country where he was living in great felicity and excellent health. This Marie-Letizia interpreted as meaning that he was dead.

Shortly after Kleinmuller's appearance, General Bertrand sent word on Napoleon's behalf requesting a cook, a doctor and a priest to minister to him in his exile. Kleinmuller having by now convinced all and sundry that Napoleon was dead, the hirers chose economy over excellence. The cook was a specialist purveyor of heartburn, the doctor a drunken quack and the priest too scared to say boo to a goose. Not the ideal combination of staff for a Napoleon requiring a delicate diet and careful treatment while suffering from perforation of the pylorus by a peptic ulcer — failing which he would need the consolations of religion.

Under the ministrations of these experts, Napoleon keeled over as swiftly as if he had been shot. In the words of the veteran Bonapartist Colonel Santi des Odoards: 'It is only from this moment that [the Bourbons] now considered themselves firmly seated on the throne. For even when chained in the middle of the ocean, the giant who made them tremble for so long was still a bugbear and an endless nightmare.'

George Lewes

The philosophical literary agent

Not many people, having eloped with a leading female evangelical, then turn her into the most famous novelist of her time. But George Lewes did.

Like many people who later turn to literature, his early *curriculum vitae* has a restless air. He worked in a London notary's office. Then he was a medical student, but gave up because he could not bear the screams of the ill. Finally he became an actor, though without great success. In order to keep himself afloat, he took to writing articles on philosophical topics. He married an MP's daughter, became an ardent fan of Alfred Lord Tennyson, and wrote a couple of bad novels.

At the end of 1851, his friend Herbert Spencer introduced him to Mary Ann Evans, who was currently engaged on a project unappealingly entitled *Ludwig Feuerbach's Essence of Christianity*. Evans was a woman of serious disposition, who was at first put off by Lewes' habit of making jokes. But she was soon able to overlook this little failing, divining that under his wisecracking exterior lay the core of a solid citizen. A couple of years later, the pair eloped to Germany and proceeded to live in what the Victorian world chose to regard as sin. They were ostracized, which suited them fine, since it spared them a lot of small talk and left the days wide open for sessions of Deep Thought.

In 1856 these sessions resulted in Evans writing a short piece describing Staffordshire rural life. When she showed it to her paramour, he became extremely excited and took it to John Blackwood of *Blackwood's* magazine. Blackwood published it, and further instalments along the same lines; the author's pseudonym was George Eliot.

George Eliot was a bestselling author in her own time, and her lengthy and sometimes exhausting novels continue to find a wide readership. Without George Lewes, it is very unlikely that she would ever have summoned up the courage to approach a publisher.

Marquis de Livry

Who had the biggest dog in theatre history

The Comédie Française is notoriously the most solemn national theatre in the world, with the possible exception of that of Sweden. It therefore comes as rather a shock to find that it was not always thus, and that the change was effected by a Great Dane, the property of the Marquis de Livry.

At some time in the middle of the seventeenth century, this faithful animal accompanied its master to a performance of Corneille's tedious but majestic tragedy *Le Cid*. The Marquis took his seat in an armchair on the stage itself, as was the wont of noble playgoers of the time. In the pit, enthusiasts drank, fought and gambled. The Great Dane entered into the spirit of the evening. At every speech it barked like a maniac. It took an inordinate fancy to the female lead, demonstrating its affection by trying to eat her lower legs. Egged on by cheers, whistles and hunting horn imitations from the groundlings, it then chased the actors from the stage and disappeared with its noble master from history.

The theatre management immediately installed a grille between pit and stage. The actors, life and limb unthreatened, were able to devote more time to their craft and less to evasive action. In time, the grillework became an orchestra pit and the railings the front of boxes, to which the nobility was transferred from its stage armchairs. Theatre design was revolutionized; French classical theatre could now be seen in all its dignity and majesty.

Merci, chien danois!

Sir Thomas Lucy

Scourge of poachers and patron of the stage

It is a commonplace that art, like a truffle, flourishes best underground. Artists themselves are often unsure about the merits of this point of view, possibly because their aesthetic souls rebel from the spectacle of their starving children, consumptive wives, etc. But the ruling class is beset by no such doubts, regarding its oppression of the bright as a form of patronage. One of the greatest of this type of patron was Sir Thomas Lucy, blood sports enthusiast, of Charlecote, Warwickshire.

Lucy was an Elizabethan knight of considerable means, active against plotting Catholics – one of whom (Dr Parry) he managed to get hanged, drawn and quartered. He was a JP in Stratford, popular in county circles, with a powerful thirst that did little to improve his temper. What he particularly disliked were the gangs of town yobbos who would from time to time pass through his coverts, poaching his deer. As a JP he was particularly well placed to bring the full wrath of the law down on the offenders; it became well known in the Stratford area that Charlecote Park, the Lucy estate, was an unhealthy spot in which to be apprehended by the keepers.

But there are always hotheads who will not listen to reason. One such was William Shakespeare, who like many others in Stratford was in sheep. Not only did this Shakespeare play merry hell with the deer herd but he also had the immortal crust to pin up an insulting ballad on the Lucy lodge gates:

> *A parliament member, a justice of peace,*
> *At home a poor scarecrow, at London an asse;*
> *If lousie is Lucy, as some folks miscalle it,*
> *then Lucy is lousie whatever befall it.*

80

This is reputed to be Shakespeare's earliest poetic effort. Whether or not he really did write it, Sir Thomas was not amused, and Will lit out for London at great speed. Here he fell in with more bad companions, who diverted his poetic talents into the theatre.

Lucy died in 1600 after a useful, but not strictly memorable life in the squirearchical tradition. Shakespeare based various characters on him, such as Justice Shallow in *Henry V* and *The Merry Wives of Windsor*. His significance, apart from these moments of literary immortality, is that but for him William Shakespeare might not have got snarled up in the tinsel of the London stage. Instead, he might have made himself a more lasting reputation and a career of solid worth in the world of sheep.

James Macpherson

Who put Celtic literature on the map – except in England

The history of literature is full of Small Players, but few of them reached the commanding heights of James Macpherson who was born in Invernesshire in 1736, studied for the church, and became a private tutor. This occupation did not agree with him, so he became a hack in Edinburgh, churning out couplets for whoever would pay him. In 1760 he came up with a sheaf of poetry which he claimed to have translated from the original Gaelic manuscripts. Published under the title of *Fragments of Ancient Poetry*, these had a fair success. In his introduction to the *Fragments*, Macpherson mentions in a throwaway manner that the *Fragments* appeared to be part of a longer epic poem, now lost but retrievable by a diligent researcher. This announcement affected the intellectuals of Edinburgh like the introduction of a rabbit into a barrel of weasels. They immediately subscribed the then enormous sum of £2000, shovelled it over to the now gleaming-eyed Macpherson, and packed him off to find the rest of the work.

He returned from the outer fringes of Scotland bearing strange tales. He had seen volumes immeasurably ancient, bardic primers half-devoured by worms. He had conversed with hereditary minstrels in windswept *brochs*. And he had indeed found the large poem of which he had spoken earlier. It dealt (he said) with the adventures of Fingal, King of Ireland, and it had been written by a third-century fellow by the name of Ossian. Literary Edinburgh held its breath while Macpherson did his translation; when it was published, literary Edinburgh roared its approval. And the whole of Europe followed suit. Edition followed edition; and in a remarkably short space of time, Greek and Roman literature – which had

82

supplied the world with literary prototypes since the Renaissance – had been supplanted by the weird and jagged lines of Ossian, the Homer of the Highlands. Ossian's success was universal.

Well, almost universal. The Scots and Continentals thought it was terrific, but the English cavilled and demurred. Dr Johnson was particularly unimpressed. Macpherson, pausing only to publish another epic entitled *Temora*, responded with torrents of abuse. Dr Johnson purchased a knotty stick for his own protection and responded in kind. Macpherson had made thousands of pounds from his books. He therefore withdrew from the fight, tacitly admitting defeat but vociferously denying it, and embarked on a career in the public service, for which he was well qualified by his pawky disposition. He was buried in Poet's Corner at Westminster Abbey, at his own expense, the funerery equivalent of vanity publishing.

The historical consequences of this eighteenth-century nostalgic are not so obvious in England, where his fraudulence is commonly acknowledged, as in Continental Europe, where his credibility never suffered critical attack. Ossian's was actually the first poetry to redeem barbarous British culture in European eyes – largely because it made a virtue of barbarism. Had it not been for Macpherson, there would have been no *Fingal's Cave* overture, and no tartan seat covers in the Whisky à Gogo, Paris.

for the Austrian and Bavarian war wounded. The piece was to be played, for some reason, not on the Panharmonicon but by a full orchestra.

The programme was: Beethoven's 7th Symphony, played as a casual warm up to the main events; two marches played by a mechanical trumpeter Mälzel happened to have invented, with orchestral accompaniment; and finally, the *Battle of Vitoria* a.k.a. *Wellington's Victory* and the *Battle Symphony*. The orchestra was not only star-studded, but also featured some bizarre instruments. Johann Nepomuk Hummel played bass drum, Meyerbeer operated a thunder machine, and Salieri commanded the several cannons demanded by the score. Beethoven conducted. Despite the hearing aids Mälzel invented for him from time to time, he was already very deaf. In *piano* sections, he crouched behind the music stand. In *fortissimo* sections he leaped about as if on a pogo stick, bellowing encouragement.

The concert was a huge success. It was repeated four days later. Almost immediately, Mälzel and Beethoven began to quarrel about who had written the *Battle Symphony*. Beethoven claimed the credit. Mälzel pirated the score. Writs flew. Mälzel, defeated, left for London. Beethoven, suddenly and to his amazement, found himself much in demand in Vienna, which had hitherto ignored his existence. His opera, *Fidelio*, which had bombed in 1803, was revived to vast acclaim.

Before one judges Beethoven too harshly in this matter, it is worth reflecting that there may have been an element of *karma* involved. It is reliably reported that Mälzel's big moneyspinner, the metronome, is not the result of his own research but was pirated by him from a Dutchman called Winkel. Be this as it may, there is no doubt that by collaborating with Beethoven on possibly the most banal piece of music Beethoven ever wrote, Mälzel catapulted Beethoven to fame. Had it not been for Mälzel, it is possible that nobody would ever have heard of him.

Marcus Manlius

The saviour of civilization

Very little is known about Marcus Manlius, except that he was a light sleeper with quick reactions who saved Western Civilization in 390 BC.

It appears that marauding Gaulish psychopaths with huge moustaches had crept down Italy and camped around the Capitol in Rome. In the Capitol, Manlius and others were awaiting death, having made grim vows to defend the citadel to the last man. At the bottom of the steep cliff on which the Capitol stands, the Gauls sat and waited for their chance.

It was a starlit night; a sharp-eyed Gaul noticed that up the cliff there was a narrow path. While the Romans snored above, and Manlius stirred restlessly on his bed, Gaulish shock-troops crept up this path. They moved so silently that not a dog barked (this may be because all the dogs had been eaten; the siege had been going on for some time).

Living in the Capitol was a flock of geese sacred to the goddess Juno (which was the only reason they had stayed out of the *cassoulet*). The geese heard the clank and scuffle of creeping Barbarians and set up a mighty honking. Manlius, roused from a shallow sleep, bounded onto the ramparts and bashed the leading Gaul with the base of his shield. This caused a Gaulslide and all the invaders eventually tumbled base over apex to their deaths. Rome was saved, and Manlius (who gained the surname Capitolinus) was a hero.

To us, too. It is more than likely that if Manlius had slept a little more soundly, we would have been deprived of the benefits of classical civilization. These include reading, writing and central heating.

Comte de Marbeuf

Napoleon's fairy godfather

Louis-Charles-René, Comte de Marbeuf, was among many people conned by Carlo Bonaparte, the notoriously charming and extravagant father of Napoleon, so this does not at first sight make him exceptional. It is only on closer investigation that his gullibility becomes epoch-making in the purest sense.

Corsica, home of Carlo Bonaparte, was fighting (and has fought ever since) for its independence from the French. Carlo was a close ally of General Paoli, leader of the Independents. After the French invasion of 1768, Paoli fled to England, beseeching Carlo to go with him. Carlo, trusting to his persuasive gifts (and possibly also to the fact that he had an extremely beautiful wife whom Marbeuf, recently arrived with the French invaders, was eyeballing) refused. He would stay, he said, and make his peace with the French.

Marbeuf proved so susceptible to Carlo's charm that he was persuaded to ennoble him, and also to sponsor his son Napoleon (named after a pro-English, anti-French Corsican rebel killed in the recent fighting) at a French military school.

Had it not been for Marbeuf, Napoleon Bonaparte might very well have been brought up as an Englishman.

Lewis Edward Nolan

Who charged too much

Lewis Edward Nolan began and ended his adult life as a brilliant, impetuous young man with a love of horses. In view of this love of horses, it is ironic that he owes his historical importance to his having caused the Charge of the Light Brigade.

During his early career, he broke new ground by advocating kindness to horses. With the right trust between rider and mount, cavalry could, he maintained, perform 'impossible' feats, including breaking an infantry square. He wrote two books on the subject, which earned him a reputation, unfortunate among nineteenth-century cavalry officers, for being Irish and able to write.

Arriving in the Crimea in 1854, Nolan found himself in undignified retreat from a winning position, the retreat ordered by the patriotic Lord Raglan at the Battle of Alma. Over the boos and catcalls of the Russians, Nolan could be heard screeching imprecations at Raglan and the cretinous Lord Lucan. Soon afterwards, Nolan was doing more screeching, this time at Lucan alone, frustrated by the fact that Lucan was at the time adopting a policy of obeying all orders to the letter, no matter how ridiculous, in order not to be charged with insubordination. This meant that the dashing English cavalry was operating only in receipt of written orders from Lucan's boss, which usually took a couple of hours to arrive.

Then came the battle of Balaclava. The Heavy Brigade routed a large body of Russian troops. But the Light Brigade, which should have galloped in to complete the confusion, was held back. The Russians accordingly regrouped behind their guns at the head of the valley.

Lord Raglan was watching events from the hills alongside the valley. He sent Lucan an order to move forward and recapture some

English guns being removed from the heights. Since the order contained ambiguities, Lucan was unable to obey it to the letter; he therefore ignored it. After an hour, Raglan sent Lucan a nudge in the following terms: 'Advance rapidly to the front – follow the enemy and try to prevent the enemy carrying away the guns – immediate.' Nolan happened to be at Raglan's side. Crazy with impatience, he barged aside the aide-de-camp on duty and snatched the message. Pointing out to protestors that he could ride better than any of them, he galloped flat out down the steeps into the valley and thrust the message into Lucan's hands.

Lucan was puzzled. He could not see the guns on the heights, since they were hidden by the lie of the land. Also, cavalry did not attack artillery without support. 'What guns, sir?' he said to the waiting Nolan.

The guns referred to were the same ones as in the previous order. But Nolan had not seen the previous order, and the muttonheaded Lucan had probably forgotten its existence. Nolan flung out his arm and pointed – not at the guns on the Heights, but straight down the valley to the guns protecting the Russians previously routed by the Heavy Brigade. 'There, my Lord, is your enemy. There are your guns!'

Lucan, as we know, was obeying all orders without query. An ADC's command had to be obeyed as if it came from the superior officer he represented. The Charge of the Light Brigade began.

After fifty yards, Nolan suddenly accelerated and in defiance of military etiquette galloped across the line of the Brigade, in front of Lord Cardigan, brandishing his sword and yelling. Perhaps he had realized his mistake, or perhaps he had decided to call off a little practical joke. Whatever the case, Russian shrapnel at this point removed the front of his ribcage, exposing his heart. Stuck in the saddle, arm still raised, he ploughed screeching through the ranks of the Light Brigade and into history. The Light Brigade charged on to seventy per cent casualties and Alfred Lord Tennyson.

The scandal that followed began a military revolution in England, Europe and the United States. Soldiers ceased to be aristocratic part-time warriors and became professionals – educated at staff colleges, promoted by merit, properly supplied, trained and cared for. In his way the impetuous Nolan was a founder of the modern army – just as he had sparked off the cannonade whose guns sounded the final salute to the old.

Nongqawuse

The day the sun rose and set as usual

The example of Nongqawuse is one that all prospective Joan of Arcs should examine carefully before setting up shop. She was a member of the Gcaleka Xhosa Tribe, which in the mid-nineteenth century inhabited part of South Africa. In 1856, when she was fourteen years old, she was staring into the waters of the Gxara river when she saw an apparition. The faces of her ancestors appeared in the water and informed her that they were going to rise up and lead the tribes in a war against the Imperialist Europeans currently cramping their style. There were a few simple conditions: the tribe must destroy all its cattle and possessions by 18 February 1857, upon which date the sun would change direction and all would proceed as prognosticated. If the tribe failed to do as it was told, it would be transformed into insects and reptiles and obliterated by a great tempest.

Nongqawuse told the elders of the tribe what she had seen, and they took steps accordingly. It took nearly a year to burn crops, chattels and livestock, but they went at it doggedly, and by the appointed date the deed was done. Ignoring the first rumblings of hunger, they sat and waited on that breakfastless 18 February of 1857 for the sun to change direction. Unaccountably, it failed to do so. Evidently, the deal was off.

Over 25,000 members of the Gcaleka Xhosas died of starvation. Nongqawuse spent the rest of her life an expatriate in the Eastern Province, presumably wondering what had gone wrong.

THE END IS NIGH

On the previous page is a disturbing account of how this young Lady came to be.

She inherited her Great-Grandmother's Business...

92

Oebares

The kingmaker

It is well known that Darius, King of the Persians, was one of history's first empire-builders, and that without him there would have been no battle of Thermopylae and thus no New York Marathon. It is less well known that Darius owed his high position to a bit of early horse-doping carried out by the groom Oebares, an otherwise completely insignificant individual. The facts of the matter were as follows.

Oebares seems to have been a more than usually perfect specimen of those Central Asian horsecoping tribesmen who brought humanity (among other things) the snaffle bit and the Parthian shot. His master Darius was one of seven Persian nobles who in 522 BC deposed a pair of usurping Magi from the throne of Persia. The seven then entered on discussions as to who should be king, and it was decided that they would all report on horseback to a spot outside the city walls at dawn. The first rider whose horse neighed would get the crown. Oebares accompanied his master to the rendezvous. Always the perfect gentleman's gentleman, he had taken the precaution of bringing with him a hanky with which he had mopped the parts of a mare in heat. When he passed this surreptitiously under the nose of the stallion on which his boss was mounted, the stallion snorted and neighed loud and clear. From that moment onwards, Darius was King of the Persians.

Richard Penderel

Landlord of the Royal Oak

After the defeat at the Battle of Worcester in 1651 that ended Charles II's first comeback bid, his life was saved by a man whose name is classically, gloriously insignificant. Richard Penderel was a Royalist nobody from a long line of nobodies, under-stewards and woodmen to the Catholic Giffords of Chillington.

The Penderel family lived in and around Boscobel in the dense forest of Brewood. Boscobel House had been built a hundred years previously as a combined hunting-lodge and hideout for priests fleeing from the law. Riddled with secret passages, it seemed the ideal hidey-hole for a king on the run.

The entire Penderel family rallied round. When it looked as if the house might be searched, a Penderel woodman conducted the King to an oak tree nearby, in which the monarch crouched while Cromwellians scoured the area eyes down. Later, Richard Penderel tried to get the King across the Severn to Wales without success. Finally, he escorted him to another house near Wolverhampton, whence he made good his escape southward.

The utterly insignificant Penderel is therefore responsible not only for the restoration of the monarchy, but for naming a significant percentage of English public houses – a fine record by any standards.

Diamond Pitt

The glittering imperialist

The British Empire owes its existence to two types of pioneer. The type most often found in history books is the idealist, determined to open up unknown territory to political and religious enlightenment, or anyway to officially sanctioned looting. History books are understandably more reticent about those whose only ambition was to rip a broad swathe off conquered territory, and to retire rich. The second category fits Diamond Pitt like a glove.

He was born in the small, sleepy town of Blandford in Dorset, and ran away to sea at an early age. By the age of twenty-one he had set up as a merchant at Balasore in India, to the displeasure of the East India Company, who held the monopoly of trade in that quarter and from whom he had neglected to obtain permission to set up shop.

For the next ten years he dodged nimbly as the Company pursued him round the Far East. Finally the Company realized that it might as well cut its losses and gave him a job as president of Fort St George, much to the disgust of traders who, having spent most of their lives hounding him, now found themselves under his management. He eventually acceded to the Presidency of Madras.

During his time at Madras, he revolutionized trade. He started a new fashion in neck-cloths, to keep the cotton weavers employed. He also collected large diamonds. In 1701 he bought an uncut stone weighing 410 carats for 48,000 pagodas, roughly £20,000. After cutting, this was sold to the French for £135,000, to be included in the Crown Jewels.

Finally he returned to England, where he became a Member of Parliament and nagged his wife without mercy on the grounds that she had neglected the gardens of his estates. He passed a distinguished old age, sparkling with diamonds and cordially loathed by all who met him. His main legacy, apart from a vast fortune and various portraits of himself smothered in sparklers, was a reputation as the hardest-nosed businessman of his age. About the only member of his family he did not hate was his grandson, to whom he passed on much vinegary wisdom. This grandson was William Pitt the Elder, who swallowed whole old Diamond's obsession with the need for Britain to dominate world trade. It is on the grandson's interpretation of Diamond's advice that the foundations of Britain's nineteenth-century wealth (and twentieth-century identity crisis) were laid.

Mihajlo Pusara

The choral singer who started the First World War

It is well known that 28 June 1914 is the day that Archduke Franz Ferdinand was assassinated in Sarajevo. It is even better known that as a result of this assassination the First World War broke out. What is less well known is that on that day the crowds lining the Archducal route contained almost as many assassins as sightseers, and that the assassination itself was made possible by a non-assassin, chorister and juvenile lead called Mihajlo Pusara.

On the fatal date, Mihajlo was in a resting situation actingwise, and was employed as a civil servant at Sarajevo Town Hall. While he was a member of 'Young Bosnia', a secret nationalist society, he was not involved in any of its violent shenanigans; indeed, he had acquired the reputation of being a police spy. Be that as it may: he had sent to one of the most ferocious Young Bosnians, Nedeljko Cabrinovic, a newspaper clipping about the Archduke's visit in case it had escaped his attention.

Mihajlo was unable to be on the spot during the morning of 28 June, since he had to sing in the choir at the Serbian Orthodox Church. But as soon as the service was over he hurried to the Appel Quay to check out the conspiracy (he knew there were seven assassins from his organization alone spread out along the route). It turned out that Cabrinovic had heaved a bomb at the Imperial carriage, but had failed to strike lucky. The Archduke and his wife had escaped unhurt, though some of the escort had been wounded. The Archduke, sheltering in the town hall, decided to visit one of his wounded officers in the hospital. *En route* the chauffeur, baffled, took a wrong turning, fetching up opposite Mihajlo, who chanced to be standing close to Gavrilo Princip, who was yet another assassin.

97

Princip was none too bright, but he knew an assassination opportunity when he saw one. As he raised his pistol to fire, a policeman spotted him and leaped forward to grab his arm. Mihajlo, quick as a flash, hacked the policeman in the shins, putting him off his leap, and Princip fired the fatal shots. Mihajlo, the blow struck, then proceeded to his next choral engagement, at the Sloga Society.

Shortly after this, he fades into the mists of time – which is not surprising, since the effort of beginning the reorganization of Europe and most of the rest of the world is enough to make anyone fade a bit. Particularly if you do it all in one morning.

Rummy

The model waddle

Virtually nothing is known about Rummy except that he used to hang around the West End of London at the turn of the century, waiting for a horse to hold so he could earn a penny tip. His importance lies in the fact that about this time the West End was habituated by an observant infant with theatrical ambitions. The infant was deeply impressed by Rummy's walk, a ducklike waddle accompanied by a metronomic oscillation of the upper body. He learned to imitate it, and made it his trademark in his most famous role, a little tramp. His name was Charlie Chaplin: had it not been for Rummy, he might never have been heard of.

Dr Richard Russell

So we do like to be beside the seaside

Few people have left as big a mark on the leisure habits of the Briton as Dr Richard Russell. Born in 1716, he was until 1750 as anonymous a practitioner as any other in Britain. His chief area of interest was the lymphatic system. According to him, irregularities of this system could be corrected by sploshing the afflicted with seawater. Nobody argued. Indeed, when he embodied his bizarre notions in a book, *de Tabe Glandulari*, the publisher W. Owen snapped it up and translated it into English. It became an instant bestseller, running through five more editions by 1770.

Russell's favourite sea-bathing venue seems to have been the Sussex coast – first at Lewes, and then at the small village of Brighthelmstone. Sussex hoteliers and landladies, showing the acumen that has characterized their every move since, began offering facilities to health-seekers. Russell soon became known as Dr Brighton; and in 1782, eleven years after his decease, the town's continuing prosperity was sealed by the visit of the Prince of Wales. With the arrival of the Prince, Brighton achieved its present status as the Dirty Weekend capital of the world.

It is to Dr Richard Russell, enemy of lymphatic disorders and apostle of sea bathing, that each of us owes our summer holidays.

Why is this called a DIRTY weekend?

Rustichello da Pisa

The traveller's taleteller

Rustichello da Pisa, one of the world's greatest ghost-writers, lived during the second half of the thirteenth century. He was a Tuscan who earned a precarious living by retelling Breton stories about the Knights of the Round Table. Falling in with bad companions of a military type, he took to fighting against the Genoese on behalf of the Venetians. After an unsuccessful skirmish, he was captured and jailed.

His cellmate was a Venetian, wizened of visage and with a far-seeing look in his eye. It rapidly became obvious to Rustichello's trained senses that here was a man who had a story to tell. Probably motivated by the ancient hack's instinct to drag all creation down to his own level, he started nagging the cellmate to embody in prose some of the yarns he was spinning. The cellmate seems to have refused, claiming a propensity to Tired Wrist. But he agreed to dictate to Rustichello, and Rustichello commenced operations forthwith.

The result of this collaboration was *Les Merveilles du Monde*, an account of seventeen years' residence at the court of Kublai Khan; the cellmate, of course, was the celebrated explorer Marco Polo. The book received mixed reviews, some admitting its marvels and others dismissing it as purest fiction. But as History caught up with Marco Polo's travels, it became apparent that it was gospel truth. By this time, of course, both writer and ghost-writer were long dead. The book went through hundreds of editions in hundreds of languages, and is even now acknowledged to be the first serious travel book ever written.

102

Jacques Leroy de Saint Arnaud

The much misunderstood riot policeman

Nineteenth-century France, with its almost incessant round of revolution and counter-revolution, was a splendid breeding-ground for licensed thugs. It is hard to think of one who had so profound an effect on history as the otherwise insignificant Jacques Leroy de Saint Arnaud.

Jacques was born in Paris in 1801, and joined the army as soon as possible. He popped in and out of the military for some fifteen years, suppressing a riot here, running up a gambling debt there and cuckolding a senior officer elsewhere. Eventually, his spare-time activities forced him to flee France and join the Foreign Legion, putting in some valuable years of training among the burning sands of Algeria. In 1848 he was summoned back to Paris, where he suppressed a revolution; he then returned to Africa, whence he was recalled by Louis Napoleon, who wished to put himself on the throne.

The return to France from the warmth of Africa gave Saint Arnaud a permanent sore throat. This is given as the reason why, as the Imperial guard under his command faced a mob which did not wish any part of Louis Napoleon, he had a coughing fit. When the spasm had passed, he said. '*Ma sacrée toux!*' which of course means 'My dratted cough!' The Imperial Guard, however, heard it as '*Massacrez tous!*' which as everyone knows means 'Massacre the lot!' The Guard obeyed its order.

Shortly afterwards this triumph of Small Partism, Jacques leaped on to the wider stage of history (as was only just, since his cough had resulted in the sudden death of eight hundred men, women and children). Thanks largely to the massacre, Louis Napoleon's coup was a great success, and he soon declared himself Emperor Napoleon III. Saint Arnaud was sent to command the French troops in the Crimea, where he was generally conceded to be a fitting foil for the inept Lord Raglan, commanding the English troops.

Without Saint Arnaud, it is fair to say that there might have been no Napoleon III. And without Napoleon III there would have been no First World War.

Sam Scott

Appealing Dred Scott and the American Civil War

Sam Scott, who played a major part in starting the American Civil War, was born in Southampton County, Virginia, in about 1795. (Nobody is quite sure of the exact date, as no one bothered much about slaves' birthdays.) His master from birth was called Peter Blow. When Blow died, Sam was sold to Dr John Emerson, who took him to Fort Snelling (now Minneapolis, Minnesota). Fort Snelling was then in Wisconsin Territory, which was a free, or non-slave, state. Here Sam (who for reasons of his own called himself Dred) married Harriet, another of Dr Emerson's slaves, who bore him a son.

In 1843 Emerson died, leaving the Scott family to his widow Irene. By this time they had returned to Missouri, where slavery was still legal. But Dred, having tasted freedom, had no wish to lose it. He therefore started legal proceedings against Mrs Emerson, claiming that having lived in non-slave states, he and his family were no longer slaves. The case lasted eleven years, and resulted in a verdict favourable to the Scotts. When the Missouri Supreme Court, on appeal, found in favour of Mrs Emerson, Dred refused to admit defeat.

A change of ownership consequent on Mrs Emerson's remarriage gave him a chance to reopen proceedings. This time the case went to the Supreme Court of the USA, which decided by a narrow majority that since Dred was a slave he was not a citizen of the USA and was therefore not eligible to sue in the Federal Courts.

This decision infuriated Northern abolitionists and members of the newly formed Republican party, while it comforted Southern slave-owners who by this time were feeling hemmed in by pious Yankees. This heightening of emotions playd a large part in the North/ South split that precipitated the Civil War.

For the Scotts the battle ended happily, despite the blizzards of words (and later, bullets) raging over their heads. Soon after the trial their owner sold them for a nominal sum to Taylor Blow, son of Dred's original owner. Taylor freed them instantly, on 26 May 1857. Dred died sixteen months later.

Norman Selby

The Real McCoy

Norman Selby's two main attributes were attractive dimples and a powerful left hook. Using the latter, and operating under the *sobriquet* Kid McCoy, he knocked out Joe Choynski in 1899, earning brief fame as the original Real McCoy. Soon afterwards, he was knocked out by Jim Corbett in the fifth round amid rumours that he had been induced to lie down not by Corbett's fists but by a wad of notes from a gambling syndicate wishing to be sure of the fight's outcome.

It was now the turn of the dimples. After a short theatrical career and nine marriages, McCoy found himself working as a physical instructor at Gus's Baths in Palm Beach, Florida. Palm Beach was at this time a restful array of clapboard cottages and hotels on a sandbar, patronized by a potpourri of rich Americans wishing to let their hair down and take it easy. It was while he was pummelling these magnates that McCoy happened to catch the eye of the famous dancer and aesthete Isadora Duncan, who had recently arrived in Palm Beach with the sewing machine multimillionaire Paris Singer. Duncan had been Singer's mistress for many years. But Kid McCoy's dimples were too much for her, and she took off with him. This in its turn was too much for Paris Singer, who severed all connection with Isadora.

Singer had always been an enthusiastic amateur architect. Seeking to assuage his grief by burying himself in work, he enlisted the help of architect, wit and bunco man Addison Mizner and set about rebuilding Palm Beach. This they did in the style described by a later critic as 'Spanish-Moorish-Romanesque-Gothic-Renaissance-Bull-Market-Damn the Expense'. Palm Beach became all seven Wonders of the World rolled into one.

Kid McCoy and his dimples fade into obscurity at this point. But during their partnership, they had not only given the language a new phrase, but also given rise to the architectural follies that helped precipitate the Florida Real Estate Boom of the 1920s – which was in itself a 'dress rehearsal' for the Great Boom that culminated in the Crash of '29.

George Baldwin Selden

A push-start for Henry Ford

It takes a special type of man to destroy his own career by rescuing the Ford Motor Company from bankruptcy. This was the amazing achievement of George Baldwin Selden.

Selden was the complete East-coast Yankee. He fought for the Union in the Civil War, went to Yale and entered the ancestral law firm, specializing in patent law. His interest in patents stemmed from a love of matters technological. During the 1870s he occupied his leisure moments by pottering with designs for a horseless carriage. He used various fuels, among them steam, ammonia, carbon bisulphate and laughing gas. None of these was entirely satisfactory.

Then in 1879 he modified an engine to run on gasoline. Having solved the fuel problem, he applied for a patent. But on looking around him he observed that everyone seemed perfectly content with their horse-drawn carriages. A patent would have given him a seventeen-year monopoly of the horseless carriage. Why not (he reasoned) wait until the streets of Boston were entirely clogged with horse manure, and *then* begin profiting from his invention?

Meanwhile, he didn't want anybody else patenting a horseless carriage. So he used his special knowledge of patent law to *prevent* himself getting a patent. He drew out the process for fifteen years, secure in the knowledge that other inventors of horseless carriages would be sent packing, since his application precluded other registrations of patent. In 1895 he at last registered the patent for his and sat back, waiting for the royalties to roll in. And sure enough, in they rolled, from companies great and small.

Except one. It was tiny, it was brash and it was broke. It was the Ford Motor Company, and it said it was not paying royalties because it could not afford to pay royalties. Selden, incensed, sued. The press, grasping the stick firmly by the wrong end, immediately cast him as Goliath, and Henry Ford as David. Ford rocketed from obscurity into the headlines and shortly afterwards (while the case was still raging) produced the Model T. The publicity already surrounding its producer is not thought to have harmed the Model T's chances. Success enabled Ford to hire bigger and better lawyers, and in 1911 the courts decided that neither Ford nor any other automobile manufacturer was under any obligation to pay royalties to Selden. All payments ceased. Selden died broke in 1922, the year Henry Ford Sr. published his autobiography.

Alexander Selkirk

Desert island castaway

Alexander Selkirk was the son of a Scottish shoemaker and in early life showed no promise of any kind. His childhood companions would have been extremely surprised if they had known he was to be the prototype for one of the best-loved characters in fiction.

He enters history by getting himself summoned by the Kirk elders of Largs for indecent conduct in church. Reluctant to answer the summons, he ran away to sea instead.

A year later he was back, and this time the elders got him. After a public reproof for beating up his six elder brothers, Selkirk hopped it again, and this time he did it properly. He signed with a Captain Stradling, commanding the *Cinque Ports*, one of the ships outfitted by the privateer Dampier. Selkirk and Stradling did not get on. Indeed, while they were anchored off the Pacific island of Juan Fernandez, they had such a row that Selkirk flounced off the ship, claiming that he would rather be marooned than subject himself to such a skipper. On arriving ashore and observing that Juan Fernandez was somewhat volcanic and inhabited only by goats, he changed his mind. But Stradling, delighted to have got rid of him, refused to allow him back on board and shortly afterwards sailed over the horizon.

During the five years that followed, Selkirk came to know a great deal about goats. At first, he shot them. Then the gunpowder ran out, and he pursued them on foot. He dressed in goatskins, ate goats' meat, and smelt like a goat. In 1709, he was picked up by his old boss Dampier, and shipped back to Scotland, where he dug himself a cave in his father's back garden and lived the contemplative life.

After a rest he travelled to Bristol and embarked upon a career of good-humoured bigamy and assault. He seems not to have been at all

fazed by the international celebrity he achieved in 1719 with the publishing of Daniel Defoe's *Robinson Crusoe*. The author had read
about Selkirk, and used him as his starting point (though Crusoe's
actual adventures seem to have little to do with Selkirk's, at least
where goats were not involved). In 1720 he joined the Navy, and
died on board ship in 1721.

His importance is more literary than historical. He single-hand-
edly originated the castaway theme in the novel – later carried on by
the Swiss Family Robinson, Ben Gunn, and Captain Marryat's
frightful Masterman Ready. Furthermore, he inspired the first ever
Best-selling Novel. And finally, without Selkirk literature would
have had to wait until the unspeakable *Heidi* for a novel in which the
noble goat is accorded its rightful importance.

Robert Seymour

The Rip-off Papers

Perhaps the most tragic literary figure of the nineteenth century was poor Robert Seymour, from whom Charles Dickens pinched the best idea he ever had. Seymour was the posthumous son of an Islington carpenter. The young Robert showed considerable artistic talent, and bettered himself to the extent of exhibiting at the Royal Academy. The future looked bright.

Appearances were deceptive. The following year the Royal Academy refused to hang him, and like many geniuses on the way down, he fell among publishers and earned a reputation as a quick, cheap illustrator. In time he began to draw political cartoons for the *Figaro* of London, one of the predecessors of *Punch*. His reputation grew, but *Figaro* failed to pay his wages and he went freelance. After a period of frightful indigence as a home publisher he got a commission from Chapman and Hall for some illustrations. Capitalizing on this, he used the entrée to suggest that he produce a series of engravings featuring the comic adventures of a club of cockney sportsmen. These would need short captions and link passages, to be supplied by a writer.

An author proved hard to find, since no big name wished to subordinate himself to the whim of an illustrator. Finally, Mr Chapman discovered a young hack who was doing parliamentary reports. There was not much evidence that he could write, but Chapman, a publisher to the backbone, reckoned he would be cheap. So began the adventures of the Nimrod Club, by Robert Seymour, captions by Charles Dickens.

Dickens did not seem to grasp what was required of him. He wrote to his fiancée bragging that his job was 'to write and edit a new publication . . . entirely by myself'. He then embarked on a campaign of

113

chronic overwriting, and demanded that Seymour – who was after all the senior partner – make changes to suit his script. And finally he changed the title from the *Nimrod Club* to *The Pickwick Papers*. Seymour, never the jolliest person in the world, began to feel deeply gloomy.

Issue one of *The Pickwick Papers* was not a big hit. Dickens used this as an excuse to settle more comfortably into the saddle of his high horse. For issue two, he not only wrote a glutinously sentimental story about a dying clown, but insisted that Seymour completely redraw the perfectly good illustration he originally submitted. Seymour, ever the conscientious worker, redrew and re-etched the plate, finishing in the small hours of 20 April 1836. Then he walked out through the chorus of the spring dawn to the summerhouse in his garden, and shot himself through the heart.

Dickens did not delay in finding a new illustrator and completely changing the format of *The Pickwick Papers*, which were the publishing phenomenom of the century. Normally a meticulous man, he seemed to suffer an odd amnesia where Seymour was concerned. He claimed that Seymour's contribution to *Pickwick* was minimal to non-existent and repeatedly refused financial aid to Seymour's wretched wife and children.

Without Seymour, there would have been no *Pickwick Papers*, and without the *Pickwick Papers* there might have been no collected works of Charles Dickens. Furthermore, there might now be no magazines; for *Nimrod* was the direct ancestor of all the serial publications of Thackeray, Ainsworth and Trollope, and later of Conan Doyle, Leslie Charteris and Jeffrey Archer.

Ivo de Taillefer

The singer of Senlac Hill

There are not many characters who have altered not only history, but the way we perceive it. Practically unique is Ivo de Taillefer, a gigantic minstrel bellowing songs about Charlemagne. It led the decisive Norman charge at the Battle of Senlac Hill – Hastings 1066, to most students of English History.

Some would say that this does not qualify him as a Small Part; all charges have to be led by somebody. Quite so. Hold on a minute, though, and think more deeply. England was invaded from Normandy; the invasion was spearheaded by this Taillefer cove. Some years later, in 1944, Normandy was invaded from England, invasion spearheaded by a man named Eisenhower. Linguists are aware that both Eisenhower and Taillefer translate as 'Ironcutter'.

These are the mystic facts. You may draw your own conclusions.

Julien Tanguy

Godfather of Impressionism

It is a commonplace that when most of the great Impressionist painters were producing their best work, they were too poor to buy paint.
The only reason many of them have ever been heard of is because
they ran across Julien Tanguy.

He used to wander the forest of Fontainebleau and the outer suburbs
of Paris, hawking artists' materials. He fought for the Commune and
narrowly missed execution. Then he rented a tiny shop in Montmartre,
and set up as a colour-grinder. Since his materials were not of the
highest quality, he didn't attract much custom. Those painters who did
visit his shop were Impressionists, whose view of the world attracted
the same scorn as Julien (now known as Père) Tanguy's paints.

One of Père Tanguy's few customers was Pissarro. Pissarro recom-
mended his shop, on the grounds of its cheapness, to a struggling
young artist called Paul Cézanne. Cézanne couldn't afford to buy
paint for cash, so Tanguy swapped a few tubes for some paintings.
This system worked so well that the shop walls were soon covered in
Cézannes. In 1886, Van Gogh came to Paris, and Tanguy supported
him in the same way – this time in the face of the outrage of Mme
Tanguy, who pointed out that his paintings were obviously unsale-
able. Tanguy said he liked them, and Van Gogh painted two portraits of him, which reveal an avuncular cove with blue eyes, a grey
beard, and an expression of extreme goodwill.

In time, finished paintings began to outnumber raw materials in
Tanguy's squalid little shop. Debates on aesthetics began to rage far
into the night. American critics made pilgrimages. Throughout,
Tanguy continued to smile benignly, showing off his paintings and
painters with a sort of apologetic pride, as if they were children
about whom he didn't want to be boastful.

116

PISSARRO

CÉZANNE

You see, by using SMALL DOTS
You save a bloody fortune
in PAINT.

Merde
alors.

He died in 1894, mourned by all in his little circle. Had he not set up his paint-shop, Impressionist art would certainly have had difficulty in achieving recognition. And it was in Tanguy's shop that Cezanne's paintings first attracted the attention of Victor Choquet, who was to become his patron. First Tanguy, and then Choquet, undoubtedly prevented Cézanne from starving to death.

117

Johann Tetzel

Whose overindulgence led to the Reformation

The dominant figure of the late Middle Ages was the friar Johann Tetzel. Born at Pirna, near Meissen, in 1465, Tetzel proved himself a capable student at the University of Leipzig. Soon after graduating, he became a Dominican monk, proving his devotion by selling indulgences in support of the Teutonic Knights. His next career step was to be caught in adultery at Innsbruck, for which he was condemned to be drowned. But Frederic the Wise of Saxony, living up to his sobriquet, commuted his sentence to perpetual imprisonment, and he was flung into the Tower of Grimma at Leipzig and left to moulder.

Matters could have got awkward at this point, had Tetzel not already shown himself to be one of the premier salesmen of his age. Sprung from jail by the Archbishop of Mayenne in his capacity as God's Area Sales Manager, Tetzel travelled swiftly to Head Office in Rome, where he was granted absolution by Pope Leo X and instructed to begin a new campaign. Tetzel returned to work and was soon going great guns.

An indulgence was an extremely useful document. In return for a cash payment, the purchaser was excused a certain number of years in Purgatory. The cash was passed back to Rome which used it to finance, in this case, a projected Crusade against the Turks and the completion of the basilica at St Peter's. A really good indulgence-seller could shift remarkable volume, as Tetzel now proceeded to demonstrate.

He moved about the country in a custom cart, bearing a mobile pulpit with a large chest of indulgences on its left, and on its right an even larger receptacle for the donations of the faithful.

The German masses responded well. Tetzel's Indulgencemobile

was greeted by cheering crowds and the ringing of joy bells. He had a jingle, too:

> *When another coin in the kitty rings*
> *A heavenbound soul from Purgatory wings.*

This hard sell produced astonishing results. Financially, he broke all existing records by raking 2000 florins out of thrifty Freiberg alone in only two days. Other consequences were less desirable. One of them stemmed from the perfectly legitimate sales practice of selling pre-emptive indulgences, by which a simple cash payment absolved a prospective sinner from a sin as yet only in the planning stage. It seems that one knight bought an indulgence for a major robbery. He then lay up in a nearby forest, waited for Tetzel to pass by, and looted the friar's coffers.

The splendid simplicity of this crime did not for some reason appeal to Tetzel. He hauled the knight before the Duke of Saxony. The knight produced his Certificate of Indulgence. The Duke reasoned that the law was only Heaven's instrument on earth and absolution before God demanded acquittal before the law. The knight went free, to Tetzel's intense disgust.

After this, Tetzel redoubled his efforts. He was made Inquisitor, which meant that anyone who refused to buy an indulgence from him could reasonably expect to be barbecued. He also developed a new line of patter based on some new and exciting interpretations of Christianity. Among these were that he, Tetzel, was more powerful than St Peter; that his indulgences had saved more souls than St Peter, and that holders of enough indulgences did not require absolution.

Success of this order very seldom wins universal popularity, and Tetzel was no exception to this rule. His achievements attracted the attention of a strong Gloomy Gus element, headed by that Ralph Nader of the German church Martin Luther. Luther subjected Tetzel's claims to close scrutiny and fixed to the church door at Wittenburg a list of ninety-five awkward questions, suggesting that Tetzel step forward at an appointed time to answer them. Tetzel failed to do so. From this moment onwards, the Reformation begun by Luther went from strength to strength. Tetzel's health declined, and twenty months later he died.

It is one of the great ironies of history that Luther should be remembered as architect of the Reformation when Tetzel, one of the greatest insurance salesmen who ever lived, has lapsed into obscurity. Had it not been for Tetzel, Luther might never have achieved the level of public recognition he needed to take off. Had it not been for Tetzel, indeed, Europe might even now be divided into a mosaic of abbeys with their lands, the nights illuminated not by godless electricity but by rushlights, the bonfires of cottages looted by preindulged robber barons, and the merry sputter of blazing heretics.

Thrasyllus

The saviour of Caligula

Prophets and prognosticators have always had some effect on the course of history. One of the earliest and most successful was the astrologer Thrasyllus, who unwittingly exposed the Roman world to the excesses of the lunatic emperor Caligula.

Thrasyllus enters history on the island of Rhodes, where the then Roman emperor Tiberius was interviewing him for the post of Court Astrologer. These interviews took place on a clifftop, in the company of a minder whose job it was to toss unsuccessful applicants onto the rocks hundreds of feet below. Having reached the interview site, Thrasyllus keeled over in a faint. When he came round, Tiberius asked him what was wrong. Thrasyllus replied that he had foreseen something very nasty happening to him if he failed the interview, and naturally Tiberius hired him on the spot.

Tiberius was seldom happy unless he was having people flung over cliffs. Towards the end of his life the flingees tended to be members of his immediate circle who might, if left unflung, have inherited the Imperial Throne. One day when the Emperor was contemplating the flinging of a certain Gaius, kind-hearted Thrasyllus observed that Gaius stood no more chance of becoming Emperor than of riding dryshod across the Gulf of Baiae. The nickname of this Gaius was Caligula. Shortly afterwards he caused Tiberius to be smothered in his sleep, and declared himself Emperor. One of the first of the barmy acts which were to characterize his reign was to build a causeway across the Gulf of Baiae, on which he rode to and fro.

Had Thrasyllus not made his remark to Tiberius, Caligula would almost certainly have been knocked on the head early in life, and the Roman world would have been spared his atrocities.

Francis Tresham

Jacobean supergrass

One of the splendours of the Jacobean age was the excellent facilities it afforded plotters of all types. Nowadays, plotters have to operate within the grey anonymity of government departments, multinational corporations or terrorist groups. In the latter part of the sixteenth century, however, a young man of good family could really get stuck in among the conspirators and plot his way to notoriety.

Just such a man was Francis Tresham, descendant of county baronets. He had a splendidly mysterious education (he claimed to have been at both St John's and Gloucester Hall, Oxford; but college records show no trace of him, and anyway as a Roman Catholic he wouldn't then have been allowed to take a degree). He then took to hanging about with the French Embassy set, notorious then as now for its intrigues. The Nigel Dempsters of his day knew him as 'a wylde and unstayed man'. So did the authorities; when Elizabeth I was ill in 1594, he was locked up to stop him stirring up trouble if she died. He played a part in Essex's hopeless rebellion in 1601, guarding Lord-Keeper Egerton in Essex House to stop him communicating with the Queen – to the horror of even his Jesuit mentors, who reckoned that a sound Catholic plotter had no business with rank amateurs of this kidney. After this reproof, his father bought him out of the Tower of London for 3000 marks on condition that he retired to the country.

Rustication did not entirely suit Tresham. He devoted himself to his favourite book, Blackwell's *Treatise on Equivocation*, and managed to keep his plotting hand in by conspiring with a servant to swindle his father over a real estate deal.

There followed one of those brief lulls that can occur in the most plot-filled of eras. He cheered up slightly when his old plotmate

Catesby proposed sending for the King of Spain to invade England. But this came to nothing – possibly because Catesby had meanwhile thought of a better plot, which he was working on with Thomas Winter, Guido Fawkes and other citizens of like mind. This involved blowing up the Houses of Parliament with gunpowder on 5 November upcoming. Tresham was not told about this one, probably because he was a reasonable after-dinner plotter but had no track record to speak of.

In September 1605, old Sir Thomas died, and Francis inherited. This rather changed things, since Catesby's expenses were running high and finance was a problem. On 14 October, he approached Tresham with the Gunpowder Plot proposition. As so often happens, a sudden deluge of money had wrought an astonishing change in Tresham's politics. Violent revolution seemed suddenly unappealing. In addition, Lord Monteagle, who would be stationed directly above the lethal kegs at the Opening of Parliament, was Tresham's brother-in-law. On 26 October Monteagle received an anonymous letter, telling him of the plot, in handwriting not dissimilar to Tresham's. All the conspirators were arrested, except (for the moment) Tresham. But his turn came on 12 November. He confessed to plotting, but begged for mercy on the grounds that he had been a moderating influence and had tried to stop it. It is now generally accepted that it was he who had given the game away.

A lifetime's plotting showed up on his record. He was therefore executed on 22 December, and his head was spiked over the city gates at Northampton.

If Tresham had not blown the gaff, Parliament would not have survived 5 November 1605 – which in the opinion of some would have been no bad thing.

More to the point, without Tresham there would be no annual excuse for the jolly bonfire parties which delight our children and keep firework manufacturers solvent. Tresham is certainly one of mankind's benefactors.

Kermit Tyler

Tora! Tora! Tora! (Whoops!)

It was early on the morning of 7 December 1941 that Kermit Tyler, a lieutenant in training with the US Air Corps, emerged from oblivion to make the remark that guarantees his place in the annals of Small Partism. He was in the Information Center at Fort Shafter, Hawaii, at the time. The switchboard operator called him and said that there were a couple of guys who had seen something on the radar at 515th Signal Aircraft Warning Service, on the Northern tip of Oahu.

The couple of guys were Privates George Elliott Jnr. and Joseph Lockwood Jnr. What they had seen was a blip on the radar screen so big that at first they had assumed the set was out of order. Then, as the blip came closer, they got worried and telephoned the Information Center. By the time Kermit picked up the telephone it was only ninety miles away.

Kermit reckoned that they must be US Flying Fortresses on their way from the mainland. 'Don't worry about it,' he said, and hung up.

As he himself admitted later, he did not know what his duties were. 'I was just told to be there and told to maintain that work,' he said, going on to explain that he had no experience of that kind of work, but had once taken a guided tour through the installation.

Forty minutes after the phone call, the Japanese Air Force took the anti-aircraft defenses of Pearl Harbor completely by surprise. By mid-morning, half of the US Pacific Fleet was on the bottom, and its planes were smoking wrecks. By lunchtime, the US had declared war on Japan.

Meanwhile, Kermit had returned to the shadows of History whence he had come.

Alexander Ulyanov

Elder brother of the revolution

Alexander Ulyanov's life would appear at first sight to be rather too short for him to have precipitated any great events. Deeper investigation reveals that this is far from being the case. In fact, he is easily the most significant individual in the history of twentieth-century revolutions.

He was born in the city of Simbrirsk, Middle Volga, Russia, one of six children of Ilya Nikolayevich, Inspector of Elementary Schools, and Maria Alexandrovna, formerly a teacher but now a housewife. He showed great early promise, walking off with all the zoology prizes at the University of St Petersburg. Even during his summer vacation, family records show, he was happiest when preparing a dissertation on earthworms.

The following term he fell in with dubious companions. His keen intellect now focused not on wriggling microscope slides, but on politics. He joined *Narodnaya Volga* (The People's Will), a revolutionary movement, and began making bombs.

The idea was to assassinate Tsar Alexander III on 1 March 1887, the sixth anniversary of the assassination of Alexander II. But the Tsar did not apparently fancy keeping this anniversary in St Petersburg, planning instead to go to his Crimean residence and do some sunbathing. The plotters brought the date forward, and lay in wait in front of St Isaac's Cathedral. The Tsar failed to appear. A few weeks later the plotters stationed themselves on the Nevsky Prospekt; once again the Tsar pulled a No Show. The disgruntled plotters concealed their bombs under their cloaks and went drinking. But one of them had been followed by the dreaded Okhrana, the Tsar's secret police; all fifteen conspirators were arrested.

Alexander, who as the brain-box of the group had personally

I'll make them
pay for this ...
I'll ... I'll ...
I'll invent LENINISM

manufactured the bombs, took all the responsibility on himself. His mother pleaded with the Tsar; the Tsar failed to listen. At his trial Alexander held firm to the end. Vis-à-vis the death penalty, he observed: 'There is no death more honourable than death for the common good.' Death sentences were passed on all the conspirators. Those of Alexander's accomplices were commuted but Alexander's was not. His last request was for a volume of Heine's poetry. On 8 May 1887 he took the final walk.

Vladimir Ilyich, his sixteen-year-old brother, was shattered. When he read the report of Alexander's death, he flung the paper to the ground, saying: 'I'll make them pay for this! I swear I will!'

Vladimir Ilyich Ulyanov, deeply politicized by the death of his idealistic brother, himself rose to prominence thirteen years later. By that time he had assumed a new name: Vladimir Ilyich Lenin.

126

Vicente de Valverde

Who satisfied the Incas' appetite for religion

The origins of the Dominican monk Vicente de Valverde are obscure. Little is known about him, except during the few years he spent in South America, where he was responsible for the founding of most of the Spanish Empire.

During the second quarter of the sixteenth century, life was tough for a Dominican monk without connections. The easiest route to preferment lay in the New World. Vicente accordingly linked up with the looter Pizarro, and accompanied him to Peru on the promise of a large diocese, full of gold and savages.

On Saturday, 16 November 1532, a parley had been arranged between the Inca King Atahualpa and the 'whore's bastard' Pizarro, in the main square of Cajamarca. Atahualpa arrived accompanied by 6000 unarmed (but gloriously bejewelled) men. The only Spaniards in the square were Valverde and an interpreter, drab as sparrows among the rainbow throng.

It is worth noting that the Emperor Charles of Spain, when sending his conquistadores to spread the word of God (loot was seldom mentioned, somehow) insisted on the observation of certain rules. For instance, conquistadores were not allowed to start massacring indigenous races until they had first asked the said races if they would submit forthwith to the True Religion. This was not only fair, but legitimized subsequent massacres as heretic disposal.

Instead of issuing the correct form of words, Valverde delivered a harangue in the manner of Oral Roberts, concluding by passing to Atahualpa his grubby breviary. Atahualpa glanced at it and tossed it aside (the Inca experience of books at that time had been rather short). Vicente rushed back to Pizarro, who was loitering in an alley armed to the teeth, exhorted him to fall upon the heretics, and absolved him from any sin this might involve. Pizarro did as suggested.

In two hours, the town and the surrounding plain were strewn with the corpses of 7000 Incas. Atahualpa was taken alive, to be strangled and burned at the stake by his godly captors. Vicente installed himself as Bishop of Cuzco and lived in great comfort till 1541, when his old pal Pizarro was murdered by an opposing Spanish faction. Vicente fled rapidly towards Panama by sea. His boat put in at an island, however, and he was captured by natives, who subsequently ate him just as Spain, in the years that followed, ate the vast riches that Valverde had procured for it by his timely act of religion.

Dr Nathanael Ward

The greener of the world

Probably no single figure made such a large contribution to world prosperity as the nice but deeply insignificant Dr Nathanael Ward MD. His moment came in 1827, at which time he was a hard-working doctor in the East End of London, and a rather sloppy amateur entomologist.

He chanced one day to put a caterpillar in a glass jar, add a couple of blades of grass and a few pinches of soil, and screw on the lid. As is the way of amateur entomologists, he then forgot about it. Next time he looked the blades of grass were gone, eaten by the caterpillar. The caterpillar itself had also disappeared from the story. What remained was the soil and a couple of green shoots where seeds latent in the soil had germinated.

Ward observed that the moisture in the soil condensed on the sides of the jar and ran down to damp the soil again. Summoning a joiner, he caused a larger version of the jar to be made from wood and glass – in effect, a hermetically sealed greenhouse. In this, plants would thrive indefinitely, even when conditions outside were hostile.

One consequence of Ward's invention was the Victorian craze for *terraria*. This craze is experiencing something of a revival. A more important consequence came from an experiment Ward made at the nearby London Docks. He sent a Wardian Case (as he now called his devices) full of grass to Australia, lashed down on the deck of a grain-clipper. The grass arrived in top condition, and was replaced by an Australian fern renowned for its habit of committing suicide when homesick. The Wardian Case kept it in a Little Australia throughout the homeward journey, and it emerged in London green, glossy and ready for anything.

Until this time, plants sent by sea had arrived at their destination frizzled by salt spray and more dead than alive, if not actually dead. The Wardian Case changed all this – at a crucial moment. The Far Eastern colonies, devastated by malaria, received forests of quinine-bearing cinchona trees from South America. The foothills of the Himalayas, then without cash crops, received cases full of tea seedlings, the short-lived seed germinated in Wardian Cases *en voyage* from Canton. And Australia, still in its infancy, received just about every agricultural plant it now grows in shoals of Wardian Cases.

Nathanael Ward seems to have had no profit from his world-shaking invention, except the knowledge that he had saved millions of lives and brought prosperity to some of the barest corners of the globe. From the little that is known about this kind and retiring man, that knowledge would probably have been compensation enough.

Shock White and Lumpy Stevens

Fathers of bat and wicket

Cricket is not a game that takes kindly to innovators. But during the 1770s it passed through what can only be described as a crucible of change, under the influence of the inventive genius of first 'Shock' White, and then 'Lumpy' Stevens. The lives of these unsung geniuses seem linked by Fate. Both coached at Eton College; among their pupils was George Canning, later the Foreign Secretary who took England into the Peninsular War. Whether or not this was due to character-forming by Shock and Lumpy is not known, though Canning was later to write of their 'invigorating commendations'.

Shock White, a short, stout man, was one of cricket's intellectuals. Realizing that there was no limit specified for the width of a bat, on 23 September 1771 he appeared for Chertsey against the legendary Hambeldon Cricket Club carrying an instrument of his own making which was as wide as the wicket. While this was technically accept-able, his opponents kicked up a tremendous fuss. Shock sportingly stood unprotestingly as a fielder whittled the bat down to size with his pocket-knife and play resumed. Ever since that day, the width of cricket bats had been limited to four inches.

Four years after this historic event, Shock found himself on a team against Lumpy. Now Lumpy was a demon bowler. In those days, the winner of the toss was allowed to choose whereabouts on the pitch the wicket would be sited. Lumpy invariably chose a spot where there would be a fair-sized hill between bowler and batsman – the idea presumably being to mask the origin of his swinging underarm deliveries.

Fourteen runs were needed to win, and Lumpy's opponents were batting. Lumpy, ransacking his art for cunning, delivered three of the twistiest balls of his career. Each of them went straight between the

131

two stumps that were all the wicket contained at that time, missing both. Not out; the bails had not fallen. The opponents won, to the intense disgust of Lumpy's team-mates who had the vast sum of £500 riding on the outcome.

All had not been in vain, however. The £500 was irretrievably down the tube, but from then on (the lawmakers decreed) the bails rested on three, not two, stumps.

Henry Wickham

To whom we owe the planet . . . so far

There is a certain kind of person who has the knack of being in the right place at the right time. Such a man was the plant collector Henry Wickham, who managed to change the face of the Far East by remote control from Santarem, an unimportant town on the River Amazon in Brazil.

Wickham was born in 1846, and once old enough set out on a life of botany. His chosen field was pioneer planting, which involves the naturalization of plants native to continent A in continent B, where (it is hoped) they will be economically useful.

One of the great enigmas of nineteenth-century botany was the rubber seed. Ever since Columbus had first noticed Haitian Indians playing ball games, Europeans had been crazy about rubber. But the only sources were various tribes of Amazonian Indians, who collected latex from wild trees and brought it to regional organizers, quaintly known as Rubber Barons. This was no fun for the Indians, who existed in a state close to slavery. Nor was it fun for rubber manufacturers, whose raw material was frequently polluted with dirt, shrunken heads and so on. It was only natural that attempts would be made to cultivate the rubber tree. The problem was the rubber seed, which is notoriously quick to lose fertility. Attempts to convey the stuff to England had failed, the seed being pronounced dead on arrival even after passage in the fastest sailing ships available.

In early 1875, Henry Wickham was at Santarem, gazing across the brown waters of the Amazon at the green jungle on the other side, when he heard the sound of swearing. The swearer was the captain of a steamship, who had come from England heavy laden with goods, but now found that his return cargo had fallen through. Wickham realized that his steamship was faster than any sailing ship. Quick as a flash and acting entirely on his own authority, he chartered the ship and loaded it with seeds of the rubber plant *Hevea brasiliensis*. The ship then hurtled for England. There was a nasty moment at Brazilian customs, since Brazilians were by no means keen on the export of seeds in case their monopoly went with them. Wickham pointed out that his ship was full of delicate plants 'for delivery to Her Britannic Majesty's Royal Botanic Gardens at Kew'. The customs officers, unfamiliar with Kew's role as nursery to the Empire, and no doubt assuming the ship was bulging with orchids for Her Majesty's conservatories, waved him through. On 15 June 1875, Wickham arrived at Kew. Within six months, rubber seedlings were on their way to Malaya.

Rubber has formed one of the economic staples of the Far East. It was certainly responsible not only for the prosperity of the area, but also in part for the Japanese invasions of the Second World War. Indeed, it is reasonable to say that the introductions of Henry Wickham were in large measure responsible for Japanese participation in the Second World War. The Chinese Army, weakened by years of conflict with Japan (who were themselves fighting the Allies in South-East Asia), were thus unable to resist Mao Tse-Tung's red revolution. Had Chiang Kai-Shek retained power there might well have been a war between Russia and China after 1945; which might well. . .

Henry Wickham, in Santarem in 1875, may well have prevented the Third World War.

Christina Willes

The first fast bowler

Christina Willes irrevocably changed the face of modern cricket. Born in the late eighteenth century into a landowing family, her brother, John, was a keen cricketer. Brother and sister were one day practising in a barn – Christina bowling, John batting and the family dog fielding. Christina was wearing one of the wide skirts fashionable at the turn of the century, and found it impossible to bowl underarm, keeping the bowling hand close by the hip as was then the practice. In order not to get tangled up in her skirts, she had to raise the bowling hand until she was effectively bowling roundarm. This meant that the width of her shoulders was added to the length of her arm when she threw the ball, which meant that the ball left her hand at higher speed, which meant that John Willes found great difficulty in applying the willow to the speeding orb. The dog found itself fully employed at longstop, and John Willes began thinking.

Ignoring the laws of the game, John Willes adopted this style of bowling, causing a controversy beside which the bodyline issue seemed insignificant. Eventually in 1835 roundarm bowling was legalized.

135

Alexander Yorke

'We are not amused'

The court of Queen Victoria at Windsor Castle must have been one of the most tedious ever to test the patience of its courtiers. Presided over by a Queen first besotted with a Teutonic booby and then besotted with grief at his loss, it was an epic of boredom that never failed to amaze visitors who did not know what to expect. About its only sparky moments were provided by the Hon. Alexander Yorke; and it is thanks to the Hon. Alexander Yorke that this assembly of the living dead produced its only Memorable Moment.

Yorke was a short, plump man with twinkling eyes and brown hair heavily greased back from an undistinguished forehead. He habitually crusted his dress with precious stones, and those with poor eyesight always knew when he had entered a room because of the clouds of scent that floated about his person. He was the son of the 4th Earl of Hardwicke, and came from a long line of courtiers. He himself had started early, slinking into the court of Prince Leopold, Queen Victoria's youngest son, at Oxford. Subsequently he had become the nearest thing that Victoria had to a court jester.

On the evening that Yorke minced into the history books, a visiting German prince, sitting close to him at dinner, told a smoking-room story in a Teutonic undertone. Yorke roared with laughter. The Queen, who was wolfing green peas (she was an extraordinarily talented eater of green peas) looked up and asked what was so funny. Yorke acted with a dumbness amazing in so sophisticated a courtier. Instead of substituting some innocuous pun or riddle of a type calculated to make HIH do the nose trick with the peas, he retold the smutty joke verbatim.

'We are not,' said HIH, 'amused.'

Depressingly, this seems to be the authentic account. It is not

... and then suddenly, without warning, the great ship, loaded to the gunwhales with 20,000 tons of outsize ladies French Knickers, SANK and disappeared without trace

We are not amused

known what the joke was, or who the German prince was. As to Yorke's failure to cover up, it may have been that he sacrificed himself to the German prince, wishing to evade the sticky diplomatic situation which might have arisen had he bowdlerized the joke. It may equally have been that, fed up with the German, he wished to drop this one in it from a great height (but in which case, why did he not let the Hun retell the joke *himself*?). A third solution, considered by some the most likely, is that bored to near-insanity after his years at Windsor, Yorke was ready to take desperate measures to get himself out of the castle and into the history books.